Unforgettable Atlantic Canada
The 100 Must-See Destinations and Events

Harvey Sawler | Photographs by George Fischer

NIMBUS
PUBLISHING

Nimbus Publishing Limited
3731 Mackintosh St.
Halifax, NS B3K 5A5
(902) 455-4286
nimbus.ca

Printed and bound in Canada

Design: Jonathan Rotsztain
Harvey Sawler photo: Heckbert Studio
George Fischer photo: Ryan Fischer

Library and Archives Canada Cataloguing in Publication

Sawler, Harvey, 1954-
Unforgettable Atlantic Canada : the 100 must-see destinations and events /
Harvey Sawler ; photographer: George Fischer.

Includes index.
ISBN 978-1-55109-756-5

1. Atlantic Provinces—Guidebooks. 2. Atlantic Provinces—Pictorial works.
I. Fischer, George, 1954- II. Title.

FC2005.C65 2010   917.1504'5   C2009-907322-6

We acknowledge the financial support of the Government of Canada through the Book Publishing Industry Development Program (BPIDP) and the Canada Council, and of the Province of Nova Scotia through the Department of Tourism, Culture and Heritage for our publishing activities.

This book would not have been possible without the generous support from these sponsors:

Table of Contents

Nova Scotia

Magdalen Islands

New Brunswick

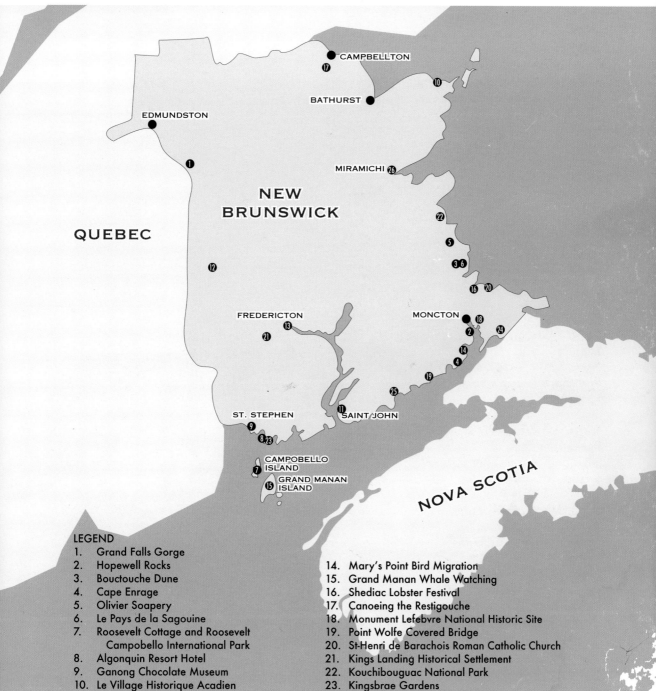

CAMPBELLTON

BATHURST

EDMUNDSTON

MIRAMICHI

NEW BRUNSWICK

QUEBEC

FREDERICTON

MONCTON

ST. STEPHEN

SAINT JOHN

CAMPOBELLO ISLAND

GRAND MANAN ISLAND

NOVA SCOTIA

LEGEND

1. Grand Falls Gorge
2. Hopewell Rocks
3. Bouctouche Dune
4. Cape Enrage
5. Olivier Soapery
6. Le Pays de la Sagouine
7. Roosevelt Cottage and Roosevelt Campobello International Park
8. Algonquin Resort Hotel
9. Ganong Chocolate Museum
10. Le Village Historique Acadien
11. Reversing Rapids Jet Boat
12. Hartland Covered Bridge
13. Fredericton Changing of the Guard
14. Mary's Point Bird Migration
15. Grand Manan Whale Watching
16. Shediac Lobster Festival
17. Canoeing the Restigouche
18. Monument Lefebvre National Historic Site
19. Point Wolfe Covered Bridge
20. St-Henri de Barachois Roman Catholic Church
21. Kings Landing Historical Settlement
22. Kouchibouguac National Park
23. Kingsbrae Gardens
24. Fort Beauséjour
25. Fundy Trail Parkway
26. Fly Fishing on the Mighty Miramichi

Ever-changing with the light, fluctuating water levels, and the four seasons, the Grand Falls Gorge is the most remarkable physical landmark on the Upper St. John River.

All along the St. John River, natural and human history compete for attention. This is especially true in Grand Falls, where a deep gorge and falls have attracted humankind since long before the site was first recognized in the 1686 writings of Monsignor de Saint-Vallier, the second Roman Catholic Bishop of Quebec. In the daily lives of Grand Falls residents, the centrally situated falls and gorge serve as the tie that binds them, a constant reminder that they share a remarkable resource. Long before the monsignor visited the area, it was inhabited by the Maliseet aboriginal people, who

named the falls Chicanekapeag, which translates as "giant destroyer," underscoring the threat the chasm has always presented to those traversing the river. One Maliseet legend has it that Malabeam, a young Maliseet girl, lured an opposing Mohawk tribe into the falls, thereby saving her village and her people.

The community of Grand Falls has gone out of its way to draw attention to their pride and joy, one of the most remarkable geological features of the entire St. John River. The site includes an interpretive centre, hiking trails, and well-fabricated stairways that descend 250 steps (70 metres or 229 feet) to the bottom of the gorge to

a spot called the "Wells in the Rocks." In spite of the steep gorge walls and perilous rocks below, this is actually one of the most accessible and safest places to explore the four-hundred-kilometre long waterway between the cities of Edmundston and Saint John. The most exciting time to witness the spectacle of the falls is during the spring freshet in April and May (weeks before most visitors arrive), when waters from the Appalachians feed the northern section of the St. John River Valley. An adventure boat ride adds to the gorge's beauty, providing an experience that cannot be found at any other location along the St. John.

Hopewell Rocks

Visitors are enthusiastic about "walking on the ocean floor" when they visit the Hopewell Rocks during the Bay of Fundy's twice-daily low tides.

"To avoid being trapped by the rising tide, YOU MUST return to the stairs by the time shown here." The sign conveying these words, and the accompanying clock, leave no doubt in the minds of visitors to New Brunswick's famed Hopewell Rocks: heed the warning or risk personal peril. It is an ominous message for a place of such beauty and wonder, but the threat, sometimes ignored by tourists, is for real. When the Bay of Fundy tides turn, they are truly a force of nature, rising to an average of 11.9 metres (39 feet) twice each day (the record is 14 metres, or 46 feet). These tides are among the highest in the world, and the Hopewell Rocks site is considered a prime place for witnessing their natural

power. Driving Hopewell's extreme tidal phenomenon is the tapered shape and gradual shallowing of the Bay of Fundy, a 290-kilometre-long oceanic funnel channeling billions of tons of water into smaller bays and estuaries in New Brunswick and Nova Scotia.

The distinctive flowerpot-shaped rock columns at the Hopewell Rocks are the result of the twisting and tilting of the earth's crust into vertical fissures that the elements—ice, rain, tidal action, and wind—have carved into their current form. The "Rocks," as the site is affectionately called, is described by the provincial government as an ocean tidal exploration site, because it is more than just a place of curiosity for tourists; thanks to tidal action and iconic land formations, the Hopewell Rocks has long been a place of considerable scientific interest.

But what draws people to the Rocks is the notion that at low tide, they can literally walk on the ocean floor, while at the opposite end of the tidal cycle, more adventurous visitors can partake in guided sea kayaking adventures. The great thing about the Rocks is that it is one of the most accessible and best-interpreted places on the Bay of Fundy. It forms part of a 2008-designated United Nations Educational, Scientific and Cultural Organization (UNESCO) Man and the Biosphere Programme region. This designation supports the claim that the Bay of Fundy is one of the world's most important coastal ecosystems. It is with this heightened sense of significance that more and more people see Fundy—and especially the Rocks—as an integral aspect of their Atlantic Canada travel experience.

Bouctouche Dune

Corporate and community collaboration and investment have served to preserve the Bouctouche Dune for the enjoyment and benefit of many generations to come.

The immense Bouctouche sand dune stretches twelve kilometres along the southeast coast of New Brunswick on the Northumberland Strait. The strait acts as a natural protector of the town of Bouctouche and its gentle bay, and is known to scientists for its important ecosystem of birds, plants, insects, mollusks, and fish. In addition to being one of the most remarkable dunes on the entire East Coast of North America, it is also noteworthy for the fact that it has been saved. Shaped for centuries by wind and sea, the dune had devolved into a playground for squatters and people riding dune-destructive all-terrain vehicles until its owner, New Brunswick's enterprising and philanthropic Irving family, began working with community interests in the mid-1990s to restore, protect, and preserve the site.

The Irving family business began in the Bouctouche area in the 1850s, and the town was home to famed industrialist K. C. Irving. As a result, the family has for decades served as a benefactor in the local area. The site was branded as the Irving Eco-Centre: La dune de Bouctouche, and is linked to a comprehensive trails network and a marina in a town which, for the most part, had seen the diminishment of most of its traditional industries of farming and fishing. Operating from a multi-purpose administrative and education centre at the most readily accessible end of the dune, Irving-employed biologists conduct wildlife and habitat research and interpreters provide programs for adults and students. Part of the centre's mission is to preserve a safe nesting habitat for the endangered piping plover. The site's two-kilometre-long boardwalk structure, rising just a few feet above the sensitive dune system, allows visitors to come in very close contact with nature without leaving a single footprint on the precious habitat. The boardwalk is so remarkable in its scale and design that it has become one of the leading photographic icons of the province.

Cape Enrage

On the calmest and sunniest of days, Cape Enrage makes believe it is a gentle place, lulling visitors with its captivating views. But do not be fooled. The Cape Enrage escarpment overlooks a place that, at its heart, is wild. The cape is formed by sheer cliffs and a rocky reef, which extends for nearly a kilometre south from the tip and generates turbulence whenever the wind and tide argue over their domain. Cape Enrage is situated at the termination point of an entertainingly winding six-kilometre road which junctures at Route 915 between Fundy National Park and Hopewell Rocks Provincial Park. The name "Cap Enrage" is attributable to early French sailors, with the British anglicizing it following the infamous Acadian Expulsion of 1755. It is a place regarded for its spectacular panoramic views of the Bay of Fundy (fog notwithstanding), forty-metre cliffs, and fossil-rich beaches, which extend for up to six kilometres. Cape Enrage also has historical importance as a Bay of Fundy light station, operating in one form or another since the 1840s. Since the early 1990s, it has been a well-known locale for experiencing professionally guided adventure sports, such as rappelling and rock climbing. The current light tower is one hundred and fifty years old and was decommissioned by the Canadian Coast Guard in 1980, but it still stands proud in the face of the harsh Bay of Fundy elements.

This jewel of an escarpment is a dichotomy of nature—one minute it can be subject to the wild winds and tidal action of the Bay of Fundy, the next minute a calm respite where visitors can contemplate nature and life.

The cape is actually the climax point of Barn Marsh Island, accessible via a permanent roadway skirting Samurai Beach and climbing to the upper escarpment; it is here where the lighthouse, lightkeeper's home (now a modified restaurant), gift shop, and adventure station are situated. The facilities at Cape Enrage were nearly lost to demolition until Dennison Tate, a Moncton-area high school teacher, and his wife, Anne, organized a group of students, rescued the facilities, and began the process of restoring, preserving, and promoting the site as both a destination and educational facility. The Tates and a continuing cycle of student recruits maintained operation at the site until Dennison's retirement from the effort in 2009. Under the auspices of a non-profit society, Cape Enrage continues to be protected, preserved, and interpreted for the benefit of both New Brunswickers and the visitors who come from around the globe to witness the phenomenon of the Bay of Fundy.

Olivier Soapery

It is playfully billed as "the cleanest show on earth," and in many ways this is true; one of the first experiences for visitors to the Olivier Soapery is the simple pleasure of washing their hands in a handsome glass basin. But there is much, much more to experience at this Economuseum destination in Ste-Anne-de-Kent, situated on a rural road half an hour from Moncton. (Economuseum network destinations such as the Soapery feature the origins, techniques, and products of traditional artisans at work.) The first thing to understand about Olivier is that the lifeblood of the business is what is referred to as a symbol of purity and life: the olive and the imported natural therapeutic oils that olives produce. In addition to the Soapery's resource library and museum, there are tours guiding visitors through time and civilizations, from antiquity to present day, on the history and art of soap-making. The main objective, of course,

is selling the dozens of soap and skin care products that are produced onsite. Olivier's official showman is Pierre Pelletier, half of the husband and wife team who created and own the business and whose live demonstrations on the use of oils, lotions, and soaps are informative, humorous, and interactive. The creative visionary behind the products is Pelletier's wife, Isabel Gagne. Together they have turned their once simple rural New Brunswick soap-making enterprise into a mini-conglomerate, with commercial outlets in various parts of Quebec, New Brunswick, and elsewhere. But the centre of their world remains Ste-Anne-de-Kent, a community close to Gagne's Acadian roots. Here she can call upon the creativity of local artists to capture the essence of her products; many of the Soapery's soap packages are mini-canvasses upon which local works of art are reproduced. Olivier has truly taken the "art" of soap-making to a new level.

Both a retail establishment and experiential destination, the self-described "cleanest show on earth" derives its theme from the healing, holistic, natural properties of olive oil.

Bouctouche-born author Antonine Maillet's 1971 award-winning book, *La Sagouine*, depicted a seemingly plain Acadian servant woman, yet one whose wisdom, wit, and charm have captivated readers and earned Maillet literary praise the world over. Le Pays de la Sagouine ("Sagouine country") was created in 1992 as an attraction designed to celebrate Sagouine and the rest of Maillet's richly crafted characters, all of whom are connected by their Acadian roots but universal in their appeal. The attraction has earned a reputation as a place for people of all origins to join in celebrating Acadia's rich heritage.

Set on the inner portion of beautiful Bouctouche Bay, Le Pays de la Sagouine looks and feels so colourful and inviting that it has become a leading visual icon for tourism in New Brunswick. Visitors are greeted at an interpretation centre and can then walk or be transported along a winding wooden footbridge that seems to float along the bay's surface, leading to L'ile-aux-Puces (which translates as Flea Island, but don't worry, there are no fleas). With its natural inner-bay setting and interactive theatrical presentations, it is an island apart from daily life. Visitors don't simply observe Sagouine and Maillet's other colourful characters; they are drawn into the comedy, drama, music, song, art, and food (with alcoholic beverages sold by a "bootlegger"). This formula of visitor engagement—from dancing to learning to play the spoons—makes Maillet's stories come ringing to life.

Acadia's most renowned literary figure—a cultural symbol of resilience, pluck, and humour—comes to life on the shores of Bouctouche Bay in southeastern New Brunswick.

Roosevelt Cottage and Roosevelt-Campobello International Park

Many find it remarkable that the late U.S. President Franklin Delano Roosevelt's summer home is actually situated in Canada. Operated under the auspices of both nations, the home and surrounding grounds form one of the most unique international parks in the world.

The Island of Campobello has difficulty at times determining whether it is a Canadian- or American-held territory. Officially the island is part of Canada, but the only way to reach the island in a car requires driving through a segment of Maine. The citizens of Campobello even have the same distinctive dialect as their Maine neighbours. Most remarkably, the island served as the summer home of U.S. wartime president Franklin Delano Roosevelt. America's beloved FDR was the thirty-second person to be elected U.S. president and the only one to exceed two terms in office (he actually served four terms beginning in 1933 before dying in office in 1945). Roosevelt cherished his summer home on Campobello, a thirty-four-room structure that today serves as the centrepiece of the Roosevelt-Campobello International Park. The president's relationship with the island began when he summered there as a boy, continued throughout his life, and was made famous in the 1960 feature-length motion picture, *Sunrise at Campobello*. More than anything else, FDR's cottage and the international park stand as a symbol of the close friendship between Canada and the U.S. The

property and its assets are governed and operated by both Canadian and American citizens, making it the only attraction in the world to be officially operated by people from two nations. The site is popular with visitors for its interpretation of FDR's life and times, and houses many of his personal artifacts. The park's gardens and nature area provide a sampler of the forests, bogs, beaches, and ocean headlands for which Campobello and its Bay of Fundy island cousins are so popular. One of the most fascinating things about the park is that it

is one of three sites in North America (the others being in the states of Washington and Minnesota) that together form an international, continent-wide sculpture entitled *Sunsweep*. Produced by artist David Barr, the sculpture consists of three black granite markers, one in each of the locations, that together are intended to represent the Canada-U.S. border. The markers serve as wonderful symbols of the ties that bind the two countries.

Algonquin Resort Hotel

There is only one thing missing when it comes to the historic, Tudor-style Algonquin Resort Hotel in St. Andrews by-the-Sea: it wasn't built directly on the sea. Otherwise, the Algonquin is as iconic an image of New Brunswick as any you can come by, having represented the province in countless travel articles and souvenir photographs. The hotel stands at the highest point in the town, and from its upper floors, you can see the local harbour and the Bay of Fundy. The hotel's magic is found in its Old World elegance and charm—echoes of fashionable women with wide-brimmed hats and parasols and fanciful couples who played croquet—all carried forward with today's gleefully painted Adirondack chairs, colourful gardens, and large New England-style porch. Although the Algonquin was originally an American idea, built by U.S. businessmen and opened to the public with considerable pomp and ceremony in June of 1889, it is a rare Atlantic Canadian example of the distinctive network of Canadian Pacific Railways (CPR) hotels built in the late nineteenth and early twentieth centuries. The castle-like hotel was a good fit for the CPR, whose hotels tended to make definitive aristocratic statements. Like its cousins in Quebec, Ontario, Alberta, and British Columbia, the Algonquin is an architectural treasure which its owners—the taxpayers of New Brunswick—continue to cherish.

The Algonquin Resort Hotel's trademark styling, wide porches, gardens, and signature Adirondack chairs make it a centrepiece of St. Andrews-by-the-Sea.

Ganong Chocolate Museum

Certain Atlantic Canadian families are associated with particular products: the Irvings with forests and fuel, the Olands with beer, the McCains with French fries and, of course, the Ganongs with chocolate. Ganong has been one of Canada's premier candy makers ever since James and Gilbert Ganong first began their family business in St. Stephen, New Brunswick, in 1873. The Ganong Chocolate Museum, on the town's main drag in what was the family's original candy manufacturing plant, tells the history of chocolate and of the Ganongs and their achievements over the generations. The museum explains, for example, that cocoa beans were used in the sixteenth century as currency and that colonists to North America in the 1700s drank chocolate for medicinal purposes. As part of the interpretation script, the Ganongs' modern-day chocolatiers emphasize that

pure chocolate is virtually free of cholesterol and salt. Ganong memorabilia includes an example of the world's first heart-shaped chocolate box, introduced in 1932 and now synonymous with romance and Valentine's Day; the first chocolate-nut bar in North America; Canada's first lollipop; and the pink, cinnamon-flavoured candies with chocolate centres first produced in 1885 and still made today—the prized treats known as "chicken bones." The museum provides an interactive learning experience—including games and videos—and offers visitors the chance to participate in a Chocolate Heritage Walk. But learning about chocolate and the Ganongs' history and heritage is merely an excuse for visiting chocoholics to share an experience with people who are devoted to the splendour of the cocoa elixir. A visit to the museum is all about sampling and luxuriating in chocolate.

A fun, interactive chocolate museum expands on the relationship the Ganong family has enjoyed for decades with Atlantic Canadians near and far. The Ganong name is synonymous within the region with Christmas, Valentine's Day, Easter, and other special occasions.

Le Village Historique Acadien

This interactive, 'living' historical village provides a museum-quality experience depicting and demonstrating the progression of nineteenth- and early twentieth-century Acadian life.

There exists a string of themed historical attractions in North America, most of them commemorating and celebrating British and French settlement or early wartime events. Yet only one accurately and elaborately illustrates the story of the Acadian people. Le Village Historique Acadien (or the Acadian Historical Village) is a professionally curated interactive indoor and outdoor museum in Rivière-du-Nord, not far from the Bay of Chaleur town of Caraquet. The village portrays Acadian life after "Le Grand Dérangement" (also referred to as the Acadian Expulsion or Deportation), which occurred between 1755 and 1763 under orders from the British Governor of the day. The expulsion saw the Acadian people forcibly removed from their lands and dispersed. Some of them gradually returned to New Brunswick, Nova Scotia, and Prince Edward Island, scratching out an existence over many generations and maintaining a unique French culture. Le Village is also different from other historical villages in that it portrays life in Acadia in three different centuries rather than at just one moment in time. Visitors can see and feel how time, enterprise, and pluck have transformed the people of Acadia. Indeed, it is the captivating arc of the Acadians' continuing story, from its tragedies to its joys, that is most intriguing: they commemorate a painful past while looking optimistically and energetically to the future.

Reversing Rapids Jet Boat

For sheer thrills you're unlikely to experience anyplace else, Saint John's Reversing Falls jet boat ride will never leave your memory. The ride departs from the Reversing Falls, a phenomenon of nature where the St. John River meets the powerful Bay of Fundy tides in a twice-daily show of physical force that is referred to by scientists as a vortex: a spiralling, whirling, unpredictably turbulent body of water. The jet boat takes people as close as they can hope to get to this wildness. The experience is delivered by a professional jet boat captain who provides in-depth knowledge of the workings of the falls. Thrill-seekers are advised to bring a change of clothes and a towel because they are certain to undergo a good soaking as the boat spins and crashes over the waves in the narrow channel beneath the Reversing Falls bridge. (As an indication that the jet boat is not for the faint of heart, there are some rules: no one under forty-two inches tall and/or under thirteen years of age can board.) The aluminum vessel is propelled by jet drives powered from diesel engines and is the

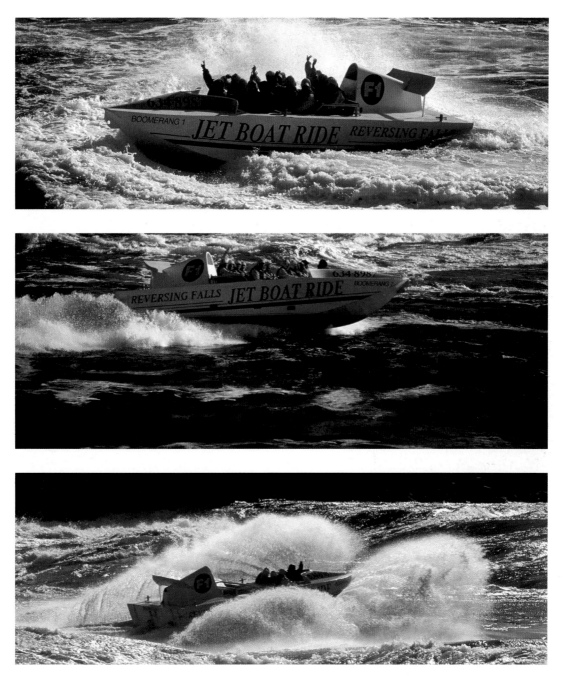

Passengers aboard the Reversing Falls Jet Boat ride in Saint John find out first-hand what Mother Nature means by the word "vortex."

only type of watercraft authorized to navigate the reversing falls, no matter the conditions. In nature's remarkable way, with the comings and goings of the moon and the ever-changing, immense tidal power of the Bay of Fundy, entering the falls is never the same experience twice. Before or after the ride and for an experience that is more passive, visitors should check out Saint John's historic waterfront, which has been transformed into a linear walkway branded as Harbour Passage, a project which combines panelled interpretation and seascapes as dynamic and fascinating as any other city in Atlantic Canada.

Hartland Covered Bridge

Forget the famed bridges of Madison County, Iowa; the Hartland Covered Bridge is the longest in the world and an unmistakable landmark on New Brunswick's upper St. John River.

At 391 metres in length (1,282 feet), the Hartland Covered Bridge is uncontested as the longest covered bridge in the world. Built in 1901, the bridge crosses the St. John River and joins the communities of Somerville and Hartland. It is one of thousands of covered bridges sprinkled throughout the world, one of more than 60 remaining in New Brunswick. (Those 60 are survivors from a list of 340 that existed sixty years ago). The loss of so many of the province's covered bridges can be attributed to the forces of Mother Nature, arson, and occasionally, neglect.

But the Hartland Covered Bridge has long been the granddaddy of them all, and in spite of vehicular accidents, damaging ice jams, and other normal wear and tear due to the elements, the local community and the provincial government have endeavoured to retain the bridge as the icon it has become. As part of this effort, it was declared a Canadian National Historic Site in 1980. The Hartland Bridge and other covered bridges in New Brunswick present romantic notions of a time past: couples have been known to stop and kiss at the halfway point. Others say that if you hold your breath, close your eyes, and cross your fingers as you walk the span, the journey will bring you good luck.

Fredericton Changing of the Guard

Evoking Fredericton's early association with the British military, the city's restored Garrison District serves as an enjoyable backdrop for the longstanding cultures and customs of the New Brunswick capital.

The birthplace of the Canadian army makes a perfect backdrop for the daily uniformed pageantry in Fredericton's Garrison District, the riverside heritage area that has emerged as the city's favourite gathering place. Designated as a Canadian national historic site, the garrison served as the compound for British troops between 1784 and 1869, and later became the site of Company A of an Infantry School Corps established in 1884. The school was one of four formed between Central and Eastern Canada and that were later raised to the status of the Royal Regiment of Canadian Infantry. Today the compound is less regimental as visitors enjoy craft shops situated within the casements where artillery was once stored. The district also includes the York Sunbury Officers' Quarters Museum, the School Days Museum, and the New Brunswick Sports Hall of Fame.

There is living, interactive evidence of the military's footprint in the provincial capital. In addition to the two poker-faced, uniformed guards who are regularly posted at nearby Fredericton City Hall, the infantry's history is commemorated twice and sometimes three times daily in the summer with the pipe- and drum-led changing of the guard ceremony in the garrison area, formally known as Officers' Square. During this ceremony, visitors are selected from among the gathering of spectators to participate in the staged inspection of the formation. After the ceremony, visitors can stroll to the suitably themed Garrison District Ale House for a cold brew and a bite.

The fields are alive with the buzz of farm machinery and bursts of blossoms as the annual potato crop takes root along the upper St. John River near the community of Drummond.

There are classic Canadian landscapes that people yearn to see and photograph first-hand: Prince Edward Island's red-and-green patchwork quilt, the dramatic Cabot Trail, the Rockies, and the Group of Seven–like images of Ontario's lakes. A lesser-known and undervalued classic Canadian landscape is the St. John River Valley and its succession of captivating backdrops. One of these is the expansive scene of brilliant potato blossoms, a New Brunswick picture postcard if ever there was one. Potato blossoms are to the St. John River Valley what vineyards are to Tuscany. While apples, citrus, berries, bananas, and pineapples are colourful, glamorous commodities that sing with taste, the unsophisticated potato—with its derogatory nickname "spud"—seems to languish in relative blandness. Planted and harvested with particular density along northwestern sections of the

St. John River, New Brunswick potatoes come in a surprising seventy varieties, including fashionable, contemporary brand names like Russett Burbank, Green Mountain, River John Blue, and Morning Gold. Such varieties are intended to compete readily in consumers' minds with the more joyous and flamboyant foods found in the local produce section.

The sun, soil, and climate in the river valley are highly suited to growing potatoes, and it is no small coincidence that areas like Drummond—at the heart of the picturesque potato-growing region—

were originally settled by Irish immigrants in the 1850s. Today's river valley population is diverse, with First Nations Maliseet, French Acadians, Danish-descended families, and those with British roots, like the McCains. The McCain frozen food empire began in the river valley community of Florenceville and originally focussed on a single product, the French fry, but has increasingly included derivative potato products such as hash browns. It is said that more than half of all the potatoes grown and harvested in the St. John River Valley make their way to the McCain Foods processing plant and thereby to tables across

North America and elsewhere around the globe. So engrained is the McCain French fry in the psyche of Canadian households that families touring through the valley can't help but take note of the company's branded emblem, just as they would for Dole along the pineapple plantations of Hawaii, for it is part of travel culture that we associate destinations and their stature with the foods and other tangibles that they produce. These things allow us to immerse ourselves in the landscape and culture of communities like those found along the St. John River—and in the tastes that linger on our palates long after the journey home.

Mary's Point Bird Migration

Like stars in a National Geographic Society documentary, thousands of semipalmated sandpipers take flight at Mary's Point on the upper Bay of Fundy. The annual occurrence is no doubt New Brunswick's most awe-inspiring spectacle of nature.

Here's a site that has more forms of protections in place than the White House. Mary's Point has received designations as a Ramsar Convention wetland of international importance, a National Wildlife Area under the administration of the Canadian Wildlife Service, and a Hemispheric Shorebird Reserve under the Western Hemisphere Shorebird Reserve. It falls within the buffer zone of the UNESCO Bay of Fundy Biosphere Reserve, and it has received the attention and investment of Ducks Unlimited. The first of these recognitions arrived in 1982 with the Ramsar designation, one of many

in Canada emanating from the 1971 international convention held in Ramsar, Mazandaran, Iran, where 158 "contracting" parties set out to conserve and protect some of the most precious places on the planet.

Occupying approximately 1,200 hectares on Shepody Bay, between Moncton and Fundy National Park, Mary's Point is a fabulous place to hike along a combination of salt marshlands, intertidal mudflats and ledges, sand dunes, and rocky cliffs. What has made the site truly famous, however, is an annual spectacle that belongs in a

National Geographic documentary film: the annual migration of the semipalmated sandpiper. This show of nature stars an estimated two million sandpipers that visit Mary's Point each August—representing 75 percent of the species's world population. The birds move in awe-inspiring flight patterns, joined as one in massive flocks that change direction simultaneously, a phenomenon aptly described as an aerial school of fish. Apart from their astounding aerial acrobatics, what's hard to grasp is how the sandpipers double their body weight during a two-week feeding frenzy on microscopic shrimp plucked from the Bay of Fundy mudflats, storing the fuel to fly non-stop to South America, a distance of more than three thousand kilometres. The very thought of such an arduous journey, especially by such a small, vulnerable creature, leaves one all the more in awe of the miracles of nature, and particularly, of the wonders of the Bay of Fundy.

Grand Manan Whale Watching

The Bay of Fundy's incredible marine ecosystem provides an ideal environment for several species of whales to feed and, in the case of the right whale, to breed. The island of Grand Manan is right in the thick of the action, providing one of the best launching points for whale watching in all of Atlantic Canada.

If you're intent on seeing wildlife during a visit to the Bay of Fundy island of Grand Manan, you could be in for an appetizer even before you arrive. It is not the least bit uncommon to see whales, seals, and porpoises during the two-hour car ferry ride aboard the *MV Grand Manan V*, which crosses between Black's Harbour on the mainland and the port of North Head on Grand Manan. These crossings and the nearby charter whale-watching experiences are almost certain to result in sightings of sea creatures, but also of bird species such as razorbills, arctic terns, and the Atlantic puffin. There are four species of whales most commonly sighted in the bay, including the mammoth humpback, the minke, the finback, and the rare North Atlantic right whale, an endangered species numbering only about three hundred, nearly all of which are known to feed in the Bay of Fundy. With the right whale in such a delicate state of survival and the other species also high on the minds of the conservation-conscious, whale-watching operators in Grand Manan and elsewhere on the Bay of Fundy practice a code of ethics that means keeping a safe distance from their sightings, as well as limiting the duration of watches. The real dangers to whales in the bay have not been from tourism, but from tangles with fishing gear and the passage of ocean-going vessels. To help mitigate whale injuries and loss of life, fishers have modified some of the apparatus they use in pursuing their catches, and the federal government put new measures into place in 2003 that regulate new shipping lanes, as well as new charts and navigational aids, to help ships veer around the giant mammals.

Shediac Lobster Festival

There is hardly a community in Atlantic Canada that doesn't lay claim to one bragging right or another: Hartland, New Brunswick, has the world's longest covered bridge and Baddeck, Nova Scotia, is the site of the first flight in Canada. Shediac, New Brunswick, not to be outgunned, proclaims itself the "lobster capital of the world," despite similar claims made by Rockland, Maine, and West Pubnico, Nova Scotia. It's not as though there are more of the popular crustaceans in Shediac Bay (situated on the Northumberland Strait) than anyplace else, but to prop up their assertion, local promoters have built what is probably the world's largest lobster sculpture at thirty-five feet in length. Situated in the town's waterfront park, the sculpture has become an irresistible photo stop for families visiting the area, joining the list of other oversized and exaggerated sculptures found throughout New Brunswick, including the largest fiddlehead at Plaster Rock, the largest fiddle at Harvey, and the largest sandpiper at Dorchester. To cap its claim as a lobster capital, Shediac hosts an annual lobster festival each July, giving visitors a timely reason to not only attend the festivities, but also to spend time at two other popular tourism spots in New Brunswick—Parlee Beach Provincial Park and Pointe-du-Chêne, both popular gathering places throughout the summer. In other words, it's really the seaside setting and festive attitude, more than the lobster, that make Shediac such a popular, must-see destination.

Fresh boiled lobster is the granddaddy of Atlantic seafood and the Northumberland Strait community of Shediac was first in the region laying claim as the Lobster Capital of the World. First come, as they say, first served.

The Appalachian Mountains wind through northwestern New Brunswick, guiding the Restigouche, a Canadian Heritage River system, to the beautiful Bay of Chaleur. Professionally operated canoe excursions maintain a respectful dividing line between the interests of nature lovers and avid salmon fishers whose private pools are as precious as gold.

Although New Brunswick's St. John and Miramichi rivers garner greater recognition, the Restigouche River, fed by the Appalachian Mountains in the province's northwest and running into the Bay of Chaleur, is of similar importance and prominence. Designated under the Canadian Heritage Rivers system, the Restigouche runs for nearly two hundred kilometres, serving as the border between New Brunswick and Quebec—from its confluence with the Patapedia River to where its mouth meets the warm bay (as its name portends) that divides northern New Brunswick from Quebec's

Gaspé Peninsula. Because it is less accessible by main roadways, the Restigouche is generally considered to be more of an unspoiled wilderness river than its provincial counterparts, making canoeing excursions there all the more isolated and adventurous. Like the Miramichi, the river is best recognized for its fabulous Atlantic salmon fishing and rustic lodges that were established by domestic and international forestry companies and wealthy individuals like U.S. tycoon William Vanderbilt. The well-established and the well-to-do still hold riparian rights, a throwback from English common

law that grants certain landowners ownership of their section of the river—this despite the fact that Mi'kmaq and Maliseet First Nations used the Restigouche for centuries before British and French settlement in the eighteenth century. So it is wise (and in the case of non-resident salmon fishing, a legal requirement) for visitors seeking out the Restigouche to engage the services of professional guides, local people who see the Restigouche not just as a waterway, but as the heritage flowing through their veins.

Monument Lefebvre National Historic Site

SPES UNICA

SJC

SJC

28
JANVIER
1895

Every culture has its special places. For the Acadian people, none is more understated, yet more important, than the Monument Lefebvre National Historic Site in the Memramcook Valley of southeastern New Brunswick. The monument is a vaunted two-storey institutional stone building which clearly evokes Catholicism, and no wonder: it was completed in 1897 to commemorate the achievements of Father Camille Lefebvre, founder

thirty-three years prior of St. Joseph's College, the first French-language, degree-granting college in Atlantic Canada. The monument also commemorates the survival of the Acadians from the time of the Expulsion in 1755 to the present day. To most Acadians today, however, it is one of the most important symbols of their cultural renaissance, captured in the Acadian Odyssey Exhibit that tells their stories of resilience and renewal. Named as a

Stained glass and other artworks capture the imagination at the site known for commemorating the odyssey of the Acadian people.

national historic site in 1994 as part of the World Acadian Congress, the building once formed part of the college, serving as a place for lectures, oratory competitions, meetings, graduation ceremonies, and theatrical spectacles. Today, the adjacent St. Joseph's College complex continues (as it has for decades) to serve as a training institute specializing in French-language immersion. But the historic site also appeals to those seeking a full-service resort experience, with dining, spas, and recreation, including a 5,900-yard golf course set against the comforting beauty of the Memramcook Valley.

Point Wolfe Covered Bridge

A family plays near Point Wolfe Covered Bridge, one of the prides of Fundy National Park. The bridge was named in honour of eighteenth-century British military figure Captain James Wolfe.

There are many under-the-surface stories and hidden gems contained in New Brunswick's Fundy National Park. One of these is the Point Wolfe Covered Bridge, an eighty-two-foot, single-span structure that crosses Point Wolfe River, a Bay of Fundy tributary. Named for eighteenth-century British military officer General James Wolfe, the bridge was built in 1908 but accidentally destroyed in 1990 by provincial road crews attempting to blast away a nearby unsafe rock ledge. Local heritage activists managed to convince authorities not to replace the span with a modern bridge design, hence the replacement bridge is practically brand new and is the only one of New Brunswick's dozens of surviving covered bridges that is painted (red).

In its heyday, the original bridge traversed the river to a settlement where loggers downed and harvested towering red spruce. The logs they felled were actually trimmed on site at a steam-powered rotary sawmill. In those days, Atlantic salmon were abundant in the Point Wolfe and the thirty-one other rivers that fed into the New Brunswick side of the Bay of Fundy. Officially declared endangered in 2001, inner Bay of Fundy Atlantic salmon have been the subject of efforts by biologists to introduce adults of the species back into the river in hope that they will spawn and start a new generation—even though the adults were born and raised in captivity. With its vantage point directly over the surface of the water, the bridge is as good place as any on the river from which to scout for the salmon as they linger in their tidal pools or manoeuvre their way up and down the waterway.

As if rising to the heavens, the simple beauty of St-Henri de Barachois Roman Catholic Church is magnified by natural light.

Age before beauty, they say. But when you have both in a single package, you have something very special. St-Henri de Barachois Roman Catholic Church is the only remaining wooden-structure house of worship in all of Acadia, giving it a rare air of authenticity associated with early French Maritime communities. (The local church, after all, was usually the centre of community life.) Built in 1826, St-Henri's simple, white exterior, single towering steeple, and Gothic windows attract the eye of anyone touring New Brunswick's Acadian Coastal Drive. Although it remains the property of the diocese of Moncton, St-Henri is no longer used for religious activities. Conserved and managed by the Société historique de la mer Rouge, its main use is as a museum exhibiting community artifacts—both religious and non-religious—and as a concert venue, the church being renowned for its outstanding acoustics. As in most houses of Roman Catholic worship, the centrepiece is the altar and St-Henri's is certainly considered a work of art in its own right. With so many aspects of Catholicism gone, the Société historique de la mer Rouge works to help ensure that the church's significance in early Acadian daily life is retained for future generations to appreciate.

Kings Landing Historical Settlement

Historic sites work best when they successfully transport people from modern day to days past. Situated on the banks of the St. John River just twenty minutes from the capital city of Fredericton, Kings Landing Historical Settlement does just that for its own historical niche—the nineteenth century. Buildings at the site are restored to a specific date so that visitors can appreciate the transition from United Empire Loyalists to late Victorians. Even while delivering on its authentic historical mandate, Kings Landing seeks to entertain, showcasing period buildings, artifacts, and stories and songs performed by in-character animators. The site's planners have also recognized that visitors love to be nourished while they learn about and experience history. One of the most popular aspects of Kings Landing is its themed Loyalist-period food and beverage operation. Relaxing in the Kings Head Tavern, visitors can enjoy honest-to-goodness comfort food and a private label beer named for Simeon Jones, a nineteenth-century Saint John brewer and businessman. The Kings Head cooks and costumed servers entertain all summer long, but it is Kings Landing's fall harvest and Christmas dinners that form its most indelible experiences, selling out to die-hard patrons year after year. And after an evening meal at the Kings Head, there are few things as warming and memorable as a wood fire, a song from one of the Kings Landing performers, a sample of chocolate toffee, and a relaxing goblet of port.

Life was austere when United Empire Loyalists settled in what is now New Brunswick. Today's Kings Landing Historical Settlement accurately depicts and re-enacts this era, but does so in a joyful, playful way through demonstrations, storytelling, music, and food.

These strands of white sand beach were protected when the Government of Canada moved in 1969 to establish Kouchibouguac National Park. The park's beaches are just one of several important habitats being conserved for future generations of New Brunswick residents and visitors alike.

The Parks Canada conservation management priority list for Kouchibouguac National Park is a complex one: there are no fewer than eighteen individual management plans, programs, and monitoring initiatives underway within this southeastern New Brunswick coastal park, set aside for protection by the federal government in 1969. Certainly there is a wealth of habitat to be managed, highlighted by the twenty-five-kilometre stretch of sand dunes. But the park also contains a highly diverse ecosystem of barrier islands, marshlands, and forests. These forests represent twenty-four tree species and thirty-seven forest types, and supports a vast list of other plant and animal life.

In addition to the park's beaches and variety of campsite types—from serviced to primitive sites, the latter of which attract true wilderness campers who love to vacation in the rough—one of the most popular activities at Kouchibouguac is the Voyageur Canoe Marine Adventure, a guided escape to the barrier islands that have formed in this part of the Northumberland Strait. Kouchibouguac provides an ideal way for visitors to appreciate the cultural and physical histories of lands and waters once traversed by the ancestors of the Mi'kmaq people.

Kingsbrae Gardens

Creativity, art, and nature combine at Kingsbrae Gardens in St. Andrews-by-the-Sea.

The sights, sounds, and happenings at Kingsbrae Gardens in St. Andrews-by-the-Sea are examples of creativity run wild. While there are beautiful gardens and fine art found elsewhere in the country, no other place in Atlantic Canada offers quite the same experience as Kingsbrae. Idyllic in its setting, with fountains, ponds, and sculptures galore, it is as much a living, breathing outdoor nature gallery as it is a horticultural experience. Showcasing more than fifty thousand plants in displays spread over twenty-seven acres, even the names of the individually themed sections evoke curiosity: traditional forms of horticulture are presented in the White, Rose, Knot, Perennial, and Cottage Gardens, with newer styles showcased in the Gravel, Edible, Secret, and Ornamental

Grass gardens. The planners at Kingsbrae truly understand how to engage their visitors. Every morning at 10:30, for example, is their Live Ladybug Release, where the bugs are set free to perform their job of preying on species that are a detriment to the gardens' roses and other plants. There are treasure hunts, croquet and bocce ball on the property's spacious lawns, and kid-targeted programs that allow adults to relax in the café and browse the gift shop. The peacocks, miniature goats, inquisitive alpacas, live and sculpted ducks, and flying sculpted geese complete the Kingsbrae visit, ensuring that anyone passing through its gates has entered an alternative world bursting with colour, imagination, and fantasy.

Fort Beauséjour

If walls could talk, Fort Beauséjour's restored remnant fortifications would relate stories of the French-British conflicts that occurred on the open, wind-swept Tantramar marshes dividing the province of New Brunswick from Nova Scotia.

At one time, the French and English stared one another down from opposing fortifications at what today is the New Brunswick–Nova Scotia border. The two properties—Fort Lawrence on the Nova Scotia side and Fort Beauséjour on the New Brunswick side—are situated on the isthmus of Chignecto, more commonly known as the barren, windswept Tantramar Marsh, for centuries a natural passageway for the area's Aboriginal peoples, the Europeans who followed, and modern travellers on today's Trans-Canada Highway. Fort Lawrence served as the British fortress, and it played a key role in the occupation and victory over French-held territories on the continent and the subsequent expulsion of the Acadians in 1755. On June 4 of that year, after a four-year stalemate, a force of British troops and New England militia attacked French-held Fort Beauséjour. Twelve days later they overwhelmed the French troops and took over the site, renaming it Fort Cumberland. Of the two original fortresses, Beauséjour is the survivor, designated by Parks Canada a national historic site in 1926. Fort Lawrence, meanwhile, is the site of a modern Nova Scotia visitor centre. Although it seems less like a fortress and more like a park with grass-covered mounds, Fort Beauséjour is a lasting symbol of French-British warfare and a site that takes in a vista of Tantramar and the nearby Bay of Fundy like few other locations.

Fundy Trail Parkway

Arguably the best-designed, most versatile destination of its type in Atlantic Canada, the Fundy Trail Parkway is at once a storied place, a touring thoroughfare, a cycling circuit, a marine park, and a haven for all levels of hikers.

Access to nature's wonders is always a delicate matter for scientists and conservationists. Thankfully, the imaginative minds behind the Fundy Trail Parkway have created the right balance of access and preservation, and in doing so, have unveiled the largest section of undeveloped coastal land between Florida and Labrador. By 2010, the parkway will extend seventeen kilometres north from the Bay of Fundy community of St. Martins and when completed in 2013 (subject to funding)

will allow visitors to connect to the southern entry to Fundy National Park by car, bike, or for the truly adventurous, foot. The parkway is a unique combination of hiking and cycling paths, seascape viewing platforms, access-ways to beaches, waterfalls, estuaries, and forests, and most remarkably, a modern touring experience. In addition to nature's master design, the project's human design considerations invite visitors to explore, learn, and relax in ways not often seen

in outdoor parks (for example, the parkway is wheelchair-friendly). Near the parkway's halfway point, the Big Salmon River serves as the site of a modern interpretive centre that relates stories of the area's once-vibrant fishing, logging, and shipbuilding enterprises. The parkway also forms an important part of the buffer zone of the UNESCO Fundy World Biosphere, placing it in the upper echelon of the world's natural spaces.

There is a definitive culture—or sub-culture one might say—connected to fly-fishing on the mighty Miramichi River and its various branches. The sub-culture consists of local guides, each with their own stories and histories of the river; of fly-tying craftsmen, each with their own style; of the lodge and camp owners along the river; of riparian rights to fishing exclusivity that is derived from old English law; of places like McCloskey's General Store near Doaktown, a curious trip down rural memory lane. These colloquial attractions tend to belie the true international significance of the Miramichi River. For decades the river has been one of the most sought-after fishing locales on the planet. Royalty, politicians, and celebrities have all flocked to south-central New Brunswick to cast their aspirations in this salmon river of choice. Long before the celebrity culture placed its stamp on the river's famous lodges (the Miramichi River's fishing culture dates back at least thirty centuries), the ancestors of today's Mi'kmaq First Nations fished Atlantic salmon and giant sturgeon at Metepenagiag.

At the heart of the Miramichi story is the famous Atlantic salmon, studied and celebrated at the Atlantic Salmon Museum in Doaktown.

Here visitors can learn about how this remarkable fish annually travels four thousand kilometres to feeding grounds near Greenland, only to return to its Miramichi birthplace to spawn—clearly one of nature's most astounding phenomena.

It is a subculture that has existed for generations: the anglers from around the world who would rather be salmon fishing on the Miramichi River than be anyplace else.

Prince Edward Island

CAVENDISH

SUMMERSIDE

CHARLOTTETOWN

BORDEN

N

LEGEND

1. Cavendish Beach
2. Anne of Green Gables Musical
3. Green Gables
4. New Glasgow Lobster Suppers
5. Malpeque Oysters
6. North Cape
7. Island Blue Mussels—St. Peters Bay
8. West Point Lighthouse
9. Province House
10. Confederation Bridge
11. Kildare Capes
12. Heritage Strawberry Social
13. Charlottetown Festival Young Company
14. Avonlea Village
15. North Rustico Harbour Deep-Sea Fishing
16. Panmure Island
17. Orwell Corner Pioneer Village

Prince Edward Island National Park stretches across the entire central north shore of the Island, enveloping kilometre after kilometre of towering white sand dunes. Among the park's many assets, none is more famous than Cavendish Beach, which has come to represent summer and

beach fun for generations of Island residents and visitors. Certainly the attractions, restaurants, gift shops, and accommodations that have sprung up near the beach reflect that family vacation theme. But in recent years the Cavendish experience has begun to shift. Golf is now closely associated

Prince Edward Island's most famous and popular beach is also one of its most fragile habitats. Counter-balancing the potential impact of the tens of thousands who visit Cavendish Beach each year, Parks Canada has designed infrastructure, such as dune boardwalks, aimed at minimizing the human footprint while still making the destination accessible.

with Cavendish and Parks Canada has installed several kilometres of paved cycling trails. But like its lesser-known cousins Brackley, Stanhope, Dalvay, and Greenwich, Cavendish Beach is more than just a seaside playground: it is a highly complex ecosystem of sand dunes, barrier islands, sandspits, and wetlands home to more than three hundred species of birds, animals such as the red fox, and a wide variety of plants. Established in 1937, the park protects part of what is referred to by scientists as the Maritime Plain Natural Region. Scientists also explain that Cavendish and the

other white-sand, north shore beaches of P.E.I. would not exist at all if not for the phenomenon of wind and tides at North Cape, more than a hundred kilometres away at the Island's western tip. The dunes are an accumulation of sand from eroding sandstone held together by a living net formed by the roots of marram grass, the blade-like vegetation that can be wicked on bare feet. Perhaps that is the grass's only natural form of protection from the human footprint. Parks Canada claims studies have shown that as few as ten footsteps across a marram grass colony can destroy its integrity, underlying the very need for the protective and conservationist roles of the national park in the first place.

Anne of Green Gables Musical

From the imagination of L. M. Montgomery, to the pages of her 1908 novel, to the Main Stage of the Charlottetown Festival, *Anne of Green Gables* endures as Prince Edward Island's best-loved international symbol.

Under the pen of world-famous children's author Lucy Maud Montgomery, Matthew Cuthbert died just once. But in the musical stage adaptation of Montgomery's novel, *Anne of Green Gables*, Anne's beloved Matthew has passed on thousands of times. And for each performance, Kleenex is at hand even for the most seasoned and hearty Anne fans. For although *Anne of Green Gables* is a mostly whimsical romp through orphan Anne Shirley's life in the fictitious community of Avonlea, the story does have its brief moments of drama, especially Matthew's tearful farewell in the show's final act.

But such times of sadness are counterbalanced with scenes like Anne tasting ice cream for the first time. The "delectable" ice cream scene has given audiences just as much joy as Matthew's death has given them tears.

Published as a novel in 1908 and staged for the first time during the inaugural year of the Charlottetown Festival in 1965, *Anne of Green Gables* endures, as Mark Twain is said to have coined it, as "the sweetest creation of child life yet written." Seen by more people than any other original Canadian musical, *Anne* has

toured nationally and, in its early years, was also presented in New York City, in London's West End, and at the 1970 World's Fair in Osaka Japan. The musical remains the standard bearer at the annual Charlottetown Festival at Confederation Centre of the Arts, running from June through September in repertory with any number of other musicals. The production has also served as the launching pad for the careers of countless Canadian actors, dancers, singers, musicians, directors, choreographers, and theatrical technical personnel. In its earliest days, the *Anne* musical—along with the Shaw and Stratford theatre festivals—fed the Canadian star system, including the centre of Canadian English-language entertainment, Toronto, and much of the variety entertainment programming of the Canadian Broadcasting Corporation.

Green Gables

For dedicated followers of L. M. Montgomery's timeless 1908 novel, *Anne of Green Gables*, one Victorian-era structure captures their imaginations. Green Gables House is the modest yet iconic location where many of the book's noteworthy events are set. Even though it has no tangible historic relevance, the building has been proclaimed part of a Parks Canada national historic site that was dedicated to Montgomery in 2005. The house and surrounding farm, owned in the nineteenth century by David Jr. and Margaret Macneill, cousins of Montgomery's grandfather, is a place where the author played as a young girl. Upon her death, Montgomery was waked for several days in the living room of the house.

Demand to visit the tiny house has been so strong—at times surpassing five thousand visitors per day—that Parks Canada was compelled to redesign and update the property several years ago by building a new interpretive facility that also controls the flow of people through the site. The newly built replica of the Macneill barn houses the L. M. Montgomery Theatre, which features the award-winning biographical film *A Celebration of Imagination—the Life of L. M. Montgomery*. After all, if one is going to spend time visiting Anne at the place she is most associated with, one will want to come away with the most complete understanding of Montgomery's rise as an international literary figure.

A simple and understated traditional farm home, Green Gables House in Cavendish is not only a mecca for fans of the perennially popular novel, *Anne of Green Gables*, but also a symbol of Island rural life.

There was a time when everything in society seemed more earnest, more real, and less expensive. This is when the traditional P.E.I. community lobster supper had its heyday. The first of these was the New Glasgow Lobster Suppers,

an enterprise that opened in June of 1958. At that time, customers paid just $1.50 for a full-course lobster meal that was plated and served by the New Glasgow and District Junior Farmers Organization as a fundraiser. Inside a modest building that had

You know whenever a queue forms, the food has got to be good. Patrons have been lining up to enjoy the experience at P.E.I.'s New Glasgow Lobster Suppers for more than half a century.

been hauled to the banks of the Clyde River in New Glasgow, the junior farmers served their meals on doors and sheets of plywood that had been propped on sawhorses while guests sat on benches. Five years later, the pastor and his congregation at Saint Ann's Church in nearby Hope River followed suit, mounting the Island's original church lobster suppers. Then came the New London Lions Lobster Suppers and it was clear that the New Glasgow idea had become a phenomenon for which the Island would grow famous. It soon became unthinkable to visit P.E.I. without experiencing a traditional lobster supper. All three operations followed a very simple formula: operate in a community hall with plastic-covered gingham table cloths and local teenagers serving freshly cooked lobster accompanied by unlimited mounds of fresh rolls, potato salad, coleslaw, jellied salad, pies, cakes, and beverages. By 1963, the junior farmers had begun staging the dinners once per week (rather than as an irregular fundraiser) and by 1970, seafood lovers were being seated seven nights a week. Over the years, as capacity increased to accommodate hundreds of guests per night, eight of the junior farmers decided to buy the operation and make the transition to a private enterprise. At the same time, improvements to the building meant it could house a lobster pound with a carrying capacity of twenty thousand lobsters. More than five decades after the suppers began, a one-pound lobster dinner today costs more than thirty dollars (or eighty-five dollars for a four-pounder), and the cars and buses keep streaming into New Glasgow every evening from May through October. Amazingly, in spite of this nightly rush of traffic, the community of New Glasgow has retained its quiet, intimate charm, making it all the more worthy of a visit.

Malpeque Oysters

You can be seated at an upscale dining table in Toronto, Boston, or Los Angeles and find the words "Malpeque Oysters" printed on your menu. The "Malpeque" has certainly achieved excellent brand status around the world as a high-quality shellfish. Along the way, the Prince Edward Island oyster industry has become increasingly sophisticated in brand-name development, including such other varieties as Blackberry Points, Conway Cups, Lucky Limes, and, of course, the Green Gables oyster. Cultured oysters, led by the Malpeque brand, have been a staple of the provincial fishery since 1865—eight years before P.E.I. even joined Canadian Confederation—when the legislature passed a statute allowing individuals to lease specific bodies of water for the growing and harvesting practice known as "bottom cultivation." Since the 1990s, bottom cultivation has given way to off-bottom, or columned, cultivation, allowing oyster farmers to access and harvest their products more cleanly and efficiently. The Island's oyster producers have also learned how to talk the talk about nutrition, bragging that their products contain twice as much iron as traditional meat and poultry products, and are excellent sources of zinc, vitamins B12 and C, and the minerals phosphorus, thiamin, and magnesium. For oyster enthusiasts, there is nothing more gratifying than sitting with a glass of white wine or a beer, tipping a shucked shell, and sliding back a fresh Malpeque that's been chilled on ice. For others, however, eating raw oysters remains an acquired taste they'd just as soon leave to the connoisseurs, preferring instead to sample the ever-expanding and inventive selection of prepared oyster recipes, including the classic Oysters Rockefeller, pan-fried oysters, and oyster soups and chowders.

Cultured and farmed fresh from the waters of its namesake bay, the Malpeque Oyster is known and served by leading chefs the world over.

North Cape

A visit to North Cape is apt to provide exposure to two extremes of technology: the time-tested practice of a workhorse and its handler harvesting wild Irish moss on the shore, and the newest in the wildly expanding science of wind-power generation. As the northern-most point on Prince Edward Island—and the tip-to-tip opposite of East Point at the province's other extremity—North Cape is already noteworthy as a natural dividing line for the currents of the Northumberland Strait and the Gulf of St. Lawrence, as an underwater reef juts out from its red sandstone cliffs. North

The namesake of one of Prince Edward Island's four scenic touring routes, North Cape has emerged as one of the leading scientific wind test sites in Canada.

Cape has also been made popular as the furthest point of no return along the North Cape Coastal Drive, which meanders through western P.E.I. Like elsewhere on the Island, the shores of North Cape have long been appreciated for their abundance of sea-based resources. But this site has also become renowned for what simply blows and flows by: it is now a government and academic research station for wind power and a wind and tidal destination for visitors. It is a stop made more complete because of the site's themed restaurant, gift shop, a nearby nature trail, and a wind farm. Billed as "the wind energy research capital of Canada," North Cape also demonstrates the possibility of hydrogen-wind

energy, a complex system that uses hydrogen to assist in storing wind-generated energy at times when the winds are calmer. It's not often, mind you, that the wind blows insufficiently at North Cape, the prime reason why scientists chose the site to conduct their research in the first place. With sixteen wind turbines towering fifty metres at their rotor's hubs, the North Cape Wind Farm generates enough power to serve the needs of more than four thousand typical-demand households, a forerunner of developments to come in other Island locations where environmental sustainability is a growing trend.

Island Blue Mussels—St. Peters Bay

By transforming the original, natural, wild species into a cultured shellfish product—known as Island Blues—Prince Edward Island mussel farming entrepreneurs have created an entirely new industry and cherished delicacy served around the world.

The clean, cold waters of the Atlantic Ocean are ideal for growing mussels, especially in places like naturally protected St. Peters Bay in eastern P.E.I. It's here and in other saltwater estuaries around the Island that long-lines of buoys can be seen suspending strings of long mesh tubular sleeves or "socks," as they are called, that are filled with seed grade mussels. It is nearly as common today to see these sprawling mussel beds as it is the Island's signature red and white sand beaches. (From the surface, these colourful strands of buoys resemble rowing competition lanes.) It wasn't until the 1980s

that the mussel industry began to emerge, with the resulting "Island Blue" brand helping glamourize the species. Today the name appears on menus everywhere good seafood is prepared and sold, including the Inns at St. Peters and Rick's Fish and Chips and Seafood House around St. Peters Bay. Mussels have made their way into countless chowder and entrée recipes, but true aficionados and gourmets like their mussels simply steamed in good old water and butter with white wine or beer, and there is no end to the creative combinations involving such flavourful accents as onion, thyme, or curry powder, to name just a few.

West Point Lighthouse

The black and white horizontal bands encircling the exterior of the West Point Lighthouse make it one of the most immediately recognizable among the hundreds of lighthouses that dot the Atlantic Canadian coast. Standing nearly seventy feet above a delicate dune system at West Point, P.E.I., the lighthouse has served as a beacon to mariners since it was first lit on May 21, 1876. What makes the West Point light unusual is that you can stay in it overnight, making it one of the few places on the Island where you can sleep within a breath of the ocean (of the property's nine rooms, the preferred

one is the Tower Room). In the 1980s, the local citizenry decided to refurbish and commercialize the property into an inn, museum, restaurant, and gift shop, complementing the adjacent Cedar Dunes Provincial Park and a working fishing harbour that has been pivotal in the lives of local residents for decades. As with most lighthouses, West Point has its own unique history of lightkeepers and their way of life as well as stories of marine mishaps, all told through images and interpretation at the museum. But it is the dune system upon which the structure stands that makes this site all the more precious and important.

Its trademark black and white horizontal striping makes the West Point Lighthouse one of the most distinctive of the hundreds of lighthouses in Atlantic Canada.

The rumour is not true that Prince Edward Island landed in the Gulf of St. Lawrence as the result of becoming separated from Mars, the red planet. The reason for the Island's red soil, red clay roads, and red sandstone cliffs is purely chemical, explained by the form of iron oxide that coats the individual particles of the soil. The Island's signature colour is a unique calling card that makes time spent here easy to distinguish from the rest of an Atlantic vacation. The red roads are so prized that the Island has identified nearly a dozen of them as Designated Scenic Heritage Roads. A second grouping of five

Carving casually through farmers' fields and woodlots, the unmistakable red roads of Prince Edward Island always lead determinedly to somewhere. Many have been designated as Heritage Roads, each with its own unique story to tell.

is non-designated, which means they may not be as serviceable. With charming local names like County Line Road, Jack's Road, Glen Road, and New Harmony Road, they can all be found on the official P.E.I. tourism website. Walking, cycling, or driving the designated roads—and other undesignated ones like them—are some of the best ways to see the Island for what it really is. The roads meander through woodlands, fringe the perimeter of farm fields, pass rare stands of hemlock, and

many still serve today as means of transportation for agricultural vehicles. There are surprise brooks and ponds, steep hills and sharp turns, and sections where trees form canopies that create moments of peace and solitude. The use of a compass or GPS is a good idea if you're going to undertake a heritage roads adventure, but inevitably, even if you feel like you're lost, worry not: the Island's red roads always connect to main paved thoroughfares that are adequately signed and marked on the official provincial highway map.

Province House

TED BY THE CITIZENS OF CHARLOTTETOWN IN MEMORY OF THOSE
PRINCE EDWARD ISLAND WHO GLORIOUSLY LAID DOWN THEIR
VES IN THE GREAT WAR AND IN HONOUR FOREVERMORE
OF ALL WHO SERVED THEREIN
1914 - 1918
1939 - 1945
KOREA 1950 - 1953

"In the hearts of delegates who assembled in this room on September 1, 1864, was born the Dominion of Canada. Providence being their guide, they builded better than they knew." This inscription at Province House, Charlottetown, refers to the first meeting of Canada's Fathers of Confederation and to Charlottetown's great historical accident as the birthplace of the nation. Province House is the unequivocal centrepiece of the Prince Edward

Island capital and the most common reference point when giving out downtown directions. Its grounds host the province's most noteworthy war memorial, fountains, green areas, Boulder Park (where boulders from each part of Canada are displayed and geologically identified), and the building stands adjacent to the Confederation Centre of the Arts, Canada's National Memorial to the Fathers of Confederation. Province House is

The landmark centrepiece of the Island capital city of Charlottetown is also the centrepiece of Canada's birth; Province House is where the Fathers of Confederation first met in September of 1864.

still the functional legislative house for the Island's government, but it has also become a place for forms of theatre beyond mere politics. Costumed animators portraying the Fathers of Confederation and women from the 1864 era use the building as a focal point for summertime guided tours of the Confederation Conference story. (The steps of the building are used to stage mock debates among the actors portraying the Fathers, including Sir John A. Macdonald, Canada's first prime minister.) The theatrics continue when the southern face of Province House is used as the backdrop for the P.E.I. Sound and Light Show, a program staged nightly from July through September. Capping

off the cachet of this national historic site is the street that leads three blocks up a gentle slope from Confederation Landing park to the Charlottetown waterfront, providing a wonderful sense of arrival at Province House. Great George Street was once described by the late author and historian Pierre Berton as "the most important street in Canada" because it ushered Macdonald and the other conference delegates from their ship, S.S. *Victoria*, into the city upon their arrival. It's fair to suggest that, considering the events that transpired here, every Canadian should make a point of visiting Charlottetown's Province House.

Confederation Bridge

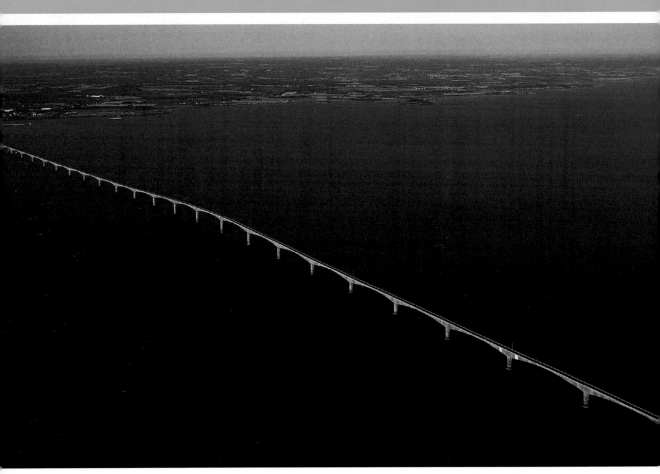

The citizenry's debate was vigorous and divisive. To diehard Islanders and special interest groups like fishers, the idea of building a bridge from Prince Edward Island to New Brunswick was all just downright silly. They argued that a bridge was certain to ravage the marine habitat of the Northumberland Strait and to destroy the Island's precious way of life. A bridge to the mainland was an idea that had been debated several times before, so it all seemed more like a ritual than serious thinking. But time and engineering finally caught up with the long-held belief that building a link to the mainland simply couldn't be done. In the spring of 1997, the 12.9-kilometre span, the world's longest bridge crossing seasonally ice-covered water, opened to much fanfare as one of

the most important technological achievements in Canadian history. At a cost of $1 billion, the toil of five thousand people connected the former Marine Atlantic ferry service town of Borden, P.E.I., to a point of vacant land in New Brunswick named Cape Jourimain. Designed to last for a century, the length of the structure called for a specialized technical design: the use of multi-span concrete box girders. The resulting structure makes for a fascinating photo opportunity, although it is illegal for vehicles to stop anywhere along the span in the interests of safety. In fact, public safety is a major preoccupation with the bridge's owners, operating under a long-term agreement with the Government of Canada. High velocity winds over the strait periodically halt the passage of high-sided vehicles, and the

A wonder of technology and transportation, the Confederation Bridge spans 12.9 kilometres across the Northumberland Strait between Cape Jourimain, New Brunswick, and Borden, Prince Edward Island.

bridge's shuttle service is a legal requirement for foot passengers and cyclists. On the Island side of the bridge, a commercial gateway village sprang up to accommodate the needs of arriving visitors, but on the New Brunswick side, commercialism was intentionally muted. Instead of the retail outlets and go-karts that greet those arriving at Borden, the Cape Jourimain Nature Centre focuses upon nature observation, conservation of the surrounding wetlands and historic lighthouse, renewable energy, and education and outreach themed on eco-responsibility. For those who miss the romance and terminal lineups of the traditional car ferries, which for decades connected the Island to the mainland, there remains a reservation-based ferry service transporting people and vehicles between Wood Islands, P.E.I., half an hour east of Charlottetown, and Caribou, Nova Scotia, near Pictou. So Islanders and their many visitors now have the best of both transportation worlds.

Kildare Capes

There is no more stereotypical Atlantic Canadian scene than the red sandstone capes that define the Prince Edward Island shoreline. Places like the Kildare Capes are "hottest"—as photographers would say—during the golden hours when the sun is low to the horizon and burning with a hue that nearly overwhelms the eyes. It is this rich tone—blended with the Island's multiple shades of green—that

visitors long to see first-hand when they arrive on the Island. The capes at Kildare look out over the Gulf of St. Lawrence along the North Cape Coastal Drive just north of Jacques Cartier Provincial Park. It was Cartier who in 1534 became the first known European to sail and chart the Maritime coastline, and there is no doubt the Island's red shores must have stood out in his mind. He may well have been

The red capes of Prince Edward Island contribute to a signature landscape that is paralleled only by the province's Gulf of St. Lawrence cousin, the Magdalen Islands.

thinking of the Kildare Capes when he purportedly wrote in his log that P.E.I. was "the fairest land 'tis possible to see."

The red capes such as those at Kildare are a quintessential item on the Atlantic Canadian bucket list, alongside the majesty of the Cape Breton Highlands and the fjords of Newfoundland and Labrador. They are to the Island what white cliffs are to Dover in southern England.

Heritage Strawberry Social

One of the most striking buildings in Charlottetown is Beaconsfield, a Second Empire and Italianate-influenced home located on the corner of Kent and West streets and designed by the Island's most prominent and celebrated architect, William Critchlow Harris. The property is situated at the eastern entry point to the city's Victoria Park boardwalk, with its porch and lawns affording a gorgeous view of Charlottetown Harbour. The building is an officially designated historic site of Prince Edward Island and serves as the headquarters for the province's Museum and Heritage Foundation. For decades, Beaconsfield has been the site of an annual strawberry social; similar socials are still held across the Island at church halls and other community gathering places. Island-grown strawberries peak during the early part of July, the perfect partner to a bowl of fresh biscuits and real whipped cream (anything short of real whipped cream is sacrilege). But the treats are merely an excuse for Islanders to do one of the things they like to do most—catch up on community goings-on and discuss local politics.

The annual Prince Edward Island strawberry harvest occurs during a very short window, in the sweet spot of summer, and compels Islanders to congregate at community gatherings for their prized strawberry socials.

Charlottetown Festival Young Company

What began as a comparably modest summertime children's theatre production at the Charlottetown Festival in the 1970s has blossomed into a full-scale production in its own right. The Charlottetown Festival's Young Company at Confederation Centre of the Arts performs, weather permitting, on the centre's exterior amphitheatre, a perfect lunchtime gathering spot for visitors. The reverberations of the production can be heard around the block as more than a dozen young Canadian performers between the ages of sixteen and twenty-three sing, dance, and dialogue their way through their signature "We Are Canadian" series of productions, which focus on a different Canadian province each year. The 2009 production, Abegweit: The Soul of the Island, told the story of Prince Edward Island's history and diversity. The show is staged free of charge but welcomes donations, which help sustain the Confederation Centre in its roles as producer of the Canadian arts and Canada's National Memorial to the Fathers of Confederation. Apart from the exuberance and quality of their live performances, what makes the Young Company program unique is that it is both a performance and training initiative for budding Canadian talent. Company members are introduced to professional instruction in dance, acting master classes, vocal workshops, mike technique, commercial voice, as well as mime and mask. Some of these apprentice performers have gone on to perform in the mainstage productions of the longstanding Charlottetown Festival, including the mainstage production of *Anne of Green Gables*.

Aspiring triple threats—actors, singers, and dancers—are showcased in the Charlottetown Festival's Young Company performances at Confederation Centre of the Arts in downtown Charlottetown.

Avonlea Village

Until a group of entrepreneurs built Avonlea Village in the famed beach resort community of Cavendish, the community of Avonlea really only existed within the imaginations of the legions of fans of *Anne of Green Gables*, L. M. Montgomery's famous 1908 novel. Avonlea—a place of post-Victorian-era propriety set against the backdrop of late nineteenth-century rural Prince Edward Island—is, after all, no more real than Anne herself. Avonlea Village is situated right in the thick of Cavendish's cluster of family attractions, but is nevertheless distinct from the collection of surrounding rides and amusements. Several of the main characters (portrayed by actors) are at Avonlea, including Anne, her beau Gilbert Blythe, best friend Diana Barry, adoptive mother

Marilla Cuthbert, and schoolteacher Miss Stacy, as well as many of the iconic physical elements of Montgomery's story, including the train station, Avonlea School, Avonlea Store, and Avonlea Church. Children can be part of the fun by dressing up in period costumes, attending Miss Stacy's classroom, and participating in memorable scenes from the book, like events from the Avonlea School Field Day. Hour-to-hour musical and storytelling presentations, together with character animations, combine to entertain visitors. There are also themed diversions like the Picnic Basket and Tea Room, an artisan studio, and a retail outlet focussed on traditional Anne souvenirs and paraphernalia.

From the imaginings of author L. M. Montgomery to the enterprising ways of Island tourism entrepreneurs, the roads and buildings of Avonlea Village come to life with costumed animators, live music, and interactive games.

There was a time when the Court Brothers enjoyed nearly as much celebrity as *Anne of Green Gables*, and were photographed by more tourists than perhaps anyone else on Prince Edward Island. Among the pioneers of the Island's deep-sea fishing industry, they represented what visitors imagined to be quintessential Maritime fishermen. It was hard to resist the unusual look of the brothers and their father; with their weathered faces and authentic fishermen's garb, they were a walking, living, breathing poster for the Island tourism industry. Court Brothers Deep-Sea Fishing remains in operation today, together with a host of other fishermen who operate out of the Acadian community harbour of North Rustico and other cozy harbours like Stanley Bridge, Malpeque, North Lake, and Covehead. With operating names like "Bearded Skipper" and "Beauty and the Beast," today's commercial tourism deep-sea fishing operators continue the tradition of welcoming guests on board and ensuring that fishing for species like mackerel and cod in the open ocean remains as fun for current generations as it has been for those past. Although each of the other deep-sea fishing captains and crews have their own unique cachet and on-board interpretation, no one quite reached the league of the Court Brothers. For decades, carloads—even busloads—of tourists have arrived at their souvenir-filled fishing shed. The Court Brothers' shed was the very last in a series of buildings on the wharf in North Rustico, and was partly converted into a retail outlet that offered every imaginable Atlantic Canadian cliché, from lobster traps to seashell crafts to corny postcards. The Court Brothers have long been prized ambassadors for P.E.I. tourism, helping to bring a traditional Island fishing village to life, and creating an experience that could not be more authentic.

Several Prince Edward Island harbours are home port to deep-sea fishing charters, but North Rustico offers the greatest variety of marine experiences and the most colourful personalities at the helm.

DO NOT ROTATE
BY HAND

Panmure Island

Panmure Island (sometimes called Panmure Head) has much in common with its home province, Prince Edward Island. Since the Confederation Bridge was built to connect the Island to New Brunswick, many diehards would argue that P.E.I. no longer has true island status. Panmure likewise lost its "island" status when the government built an artificial causeway that permanently connected it to the rest of the province in the 1960s (although at low tide, Panmure had already been naturally connected to P.E.I. by sand bars). Over time, a barrier beach and sand dunes have formed, much of which now constitute Panmure Island Provincial Park. This popular beach

For "in-the-know" visitors Panmure Island is one of those most cherished P.E.I. respites from the demands of daily life.

destination is part of the Points East Coastal Drive near the entrance of Cardigan Bay and Georgetown Harbour. Built in 1853 as the province's second lighthouse—and the first to be fashioned in the form of an octagonal wooden tower—the Panmure Island lighthouse is the most commonly recognized part of the destination. The light also had one of the earliest fog alarm marine warning systems on P.E.I. Panmure folklore includes sightings of a flaming phantom ship just off the shore. (Ghost ships are

not uncommon in Atlantic Canadian culture.) One version of the origin of Panmure's phantom ship yarn involves a young local woman who was in love with a sailor disapproved of by her parents. The couple conspired that when his ship approached, he would light three signals, inviting her to join him and find their way and their life together. The ghost of this ship is said to pass through these waters to this day.

Orwell Corner Pioneer Village

In a sense, there were several "Orwell Corners" in the settlement days of Prince Edward Island, small crossroads of commerce and community connectivity that were cherished aspects of the Island way of life. But the fabric of most of these towns gradually gave way to development, shifts in the Island economy, emigration, and changes in lifestyle. There are still villages and towns that retain a strong sense of commercial activity and community—places like Hunter River, Kensington, and St. Peters—but only Orwell Corner Historic Village captures the true essence of Island community as it felt in the early nineteenth century. Named in 1769 by Island surveyor Samuel Holland to honour Britain's Minister of Plantations, Sir Francis Orwell, the site is situated halfway between the capital, Charlottetown, and the Wood Islands ferry service to Nova Scotia. In keeping

with the best of Atlantic Canada's attractions, Orwell is not just a static historic village, with its well-curated, finely preserved buildings and artifacts. It attracts visitors in large part thanks to programming that involves its audiences, including special shows like "Sundays at the Corner," "Ceilidhs at the Corner," "The Bluegrass Gospel Show," and "Artistry In Iron." Above all, it is the restfulness and peacefulness of the place that is most rewarding. The site is a place for strolling, picnicking, and contemplating the lives of the early Scottish, Irish, and United Empire Loyalist settlers who originally inhabited the community. Orwell Corner transports its visitors to a time when neighbours and self-reliance were the order of the day and the notion of travelling to the capital of Charlottetown no doubt seemed extraordinary.

Here is one community where there is no clamour and no having to be on time. Orwell Corner Pioneer Village is both timeless and time-free.

Newfoundland and Labrador

QUEBEC

LABRADOR

LEGEND

1. The Tablelands—Gros Morne National Park
2. Western Brook Pond Fjord—Gros Morne National Park
3. George Street Pub District
4. Cape St. Mary's
5. Signal Hill
6. Jelly Bean Row
7. L'Anse aux Meadows
8. Cape Spear Lighthouse
9. Witless Bay
10. Cape Bonavista Lighthouse
11. Battle Harbour Fishing Station
12. Red Bay Whaling Station
13. Moravian Mission at Hebron
14. Torngat Mountains National Park Fjords
15. Sir Richard Squires Memorial Provincial Park

TORNGAT MOUNTAINS

14

HEBRON 13

NAIN

CHURCHILL FALLS

HAPPY VALLEY – GOOSE BAY

BATTLE HARBOUR 11

12

7 L'ANSE AUX MEADOWS

2

1

15

CORNERBROOK

GRAND FALLS–WINDSOR

10

NEWFOUNDLAND

ST. JOHN'S
3 5
6 8

9

4

PORT AUX BASQUES

N

The Tablelands section of Gros Morne National Park is one of the few places in the world where the earth's mantle has been exposed for the human eye to see, earning it the designation as a UNESCO World Heritage Site.

Gros Morne National Park in western Newfoundland occupies such a large territory that it cannot help standing out because of its diversity, offering visitors a fascinating potpourri of mountains, waterfalls, marine inlets, sea stacks, sandy beaches, cottages, inns, restaurants, and working fishing villages. Gros Morne's diversity did not go unnoticed by UNESCO, an organization that does not hand out its world heritage site designations on a whim; there must be irrefutable evidence of the site's uniqueness within a global context. Such is the case at Gros Morne National Park, where a landscape feature called the Tablelands illustrates the concept of plate tectonics, one of the most important theories for understanding the earth. The theory holds that the outer shell of the earth is made up of thin, rigid plates that move relative to each other, the cause of geological occurrences such as volcanoes and earthquakes. The Tablelands are an amazing phenomenon because you can see and touch evidence of the ocean's deep crust and rocks from the earth's inner mantle that have crept up onto the surface of the land. With its unmistakable flat, barren mountaintops, striking ochre colour, and prized UNESCO designation, Gros Morne and its Tablelands have emerged as one of the most dreamt-of places to visit in all of Canada.

Western Brook Pond Fjord—Gros Morne National Park

Visiting Gros Morne National Park's Western Brook Pond means a different experience virtually every second of the day. The reason? The site is dramatically affected by natural light. When the sun is at its peak, the contrasts of the freshwater fjord's facings are vivid and inspiring; the fine details, cracks, and crevices of these six-hundred-metre rock walls are revealed. But when clouds gather or daily shadows take their form, the fjord attempts to hide the intricacies of its glacial history, growing dark, sombre, and cold.

Surrounded on three sides by the Long Range Mountains, part of North America's famous Appalachian chain, Western Brook Pond is only a "pond" in the Newfoundland vernacular; at 16 kilometres in length and 165 metres in depth, it is far more dramatic. In geological-biological terms, Western Brook is rare, categorized as ultraoligotrophic, meaning that its ability to sustain life is limited. This scientific fact means that there is a greater delicate balance involved in sustaining Western Brook Pond than most lakes or naturally flowing waterways, a balance that the proven sustainability practices of Parks Canada are well suited to controlling and managing. Respecting this resource is also the responsibility of knowledgeable, well-seasoned hikers, who can be dropped off at the eastern end of Western Brook Pond for the start of their encounter with the thirty-five-kilometre Long Range Traverse. The hike is a four- to five-day experience unparalleled in Eastern Canada that pits those with the right outdoor skills against every imaginable challenge to be found in a Canadian wilderness setting.

The very word "fjord" denotes landscape drama, and with its towering cliffs and crashing waterfalls, Western Brook Pond Fjord at Gros Morne National Park does not disappoint.

George Street Pub District

Throngs of partygoers, the reverberations of live entertainment, and "Bugden" and "Tickle" company taxicabs line the perimeter of one of the most famous party streets in all of Canada. George Street, a pedestrian route in downtown St. John's, is renowned for having more pubs per square foot than anyplace else in the country and for the fact that the nightly revellers really don't hit their stride until midnight. The street is only open to vehicular traffic in the mornings, allowing delivery trucks to restock the crush of bars and pubs. But there is something much more exciting taking place beneath the surface of the raucous pub circuit in the Newfoundland capital: an explosion of musical talent that has resulted in one of the most exciting indie music scenes in the nation. Certainly there

It is not an urban myth; with its boundless musical energy and convivial atmosphere, George Street in the Newfoundland and Labrador capital City of St. John's is one of the greatest party places in all of Canada.

remains the unmistakable Irish influence and twang of traditional Newfoundland and Labrador music, but tradition has had to give partial way to the expansion of the province's musical gene pool with the introduction of an entirely new generation of artists. Some of these artists are far too young to be served the province's signature dark Screech rum or pitchers of locally made Quidi Vidi 1892 draft beer, but they are determined to make their way onto George Street stages. With pub names such as the Trinity, O'Reilly's, Rob Roy, Bridie Molloy's, and YellowBelly, there is no shortage of George Street venues for the incubation of Newfoundland's growing talent industry. Admittedly, George Street has an edge to it that makes it better suited for bar-goers than families, but the City of St. John's is currently formulating plans to make the street more welcoming for all ages and tastes.

It is easy, standing atop the one-hundred-metre sandstone cliffs of Cape St. Mary's, to imagine yourself as a part of composer Stan Rogers's lyrical journey to this place. "Cape St. Mary's" is an emotional tune about fog, fishermen, and friends that has emerged to become one of Newfoundland and Labrador's best-known and most-cherished anthems. People gladly drive the two hundred kilometres southwest from the provincial capital of St. John's to Cape St. Mary's Ecological Reserve, touted as one of the most accessible places in the world to see nesting seabirds. The drive past Subarctic tundra, bogs, ponds, mosses, and low-lying shrubs may sound boring, but this hard landscape has an immense beauty all its own. The reserve's claim about being close to the birds is true; if you can park your vertigo long enough to venture along a tip of land only a few metres wide, you will be greeted by a uniformed guide who will point out what's going on with the sea of feathered wildlife, wedged and nested as they are onto crags of rock. During the breeding season (April through June), the provincially run reserve is home to an estimated twenty-four thousand Northern gannets, twenty thousand black-

In spite of the urge to be as close as possible to the colony of gannets, visitors with vertigo will want to keep back from the edge of the towering cliffs at Cape St. Mary's.

legged kittiwake, twenty thousand common murre, two thousand thick-billed murre, and an assortment of razorbills, black guillemot, cormorants, and fulmars. Breeding season aside, throughout the summer and fall there are still scads of birds to see and hear. One of the most fascinating things about the cape, however, is the flock of resident sheep. They cling perilously to the grassy perimeter at the cliff's edges either oblivious or in defiance of gravity, nonchalant about the ever-present danger of tumbling toward the jagged rock formations below. Even when conditions are foggy, which it is an average of two hundred days per year, a visit to Cape St. Mary's is still a life-altering experience.

Guglielmo Marconi claimed to have received the first transatlantic wireless signal in the Newfoundland and Labrador capital of St. John's on December 12, 1901. It was described as a repetitious Morse code transmission of the letter S, sent from his station in Poldhu, Cornwall, England—2,500 kilometres away. Although the achievement is disputed by some, the Italian inventor went on to share the 1909 Nobel Prize for Physics. Signal Hill, as it became known, is surely high enough and there are no obstructions between the site and Great Britain. Most visitors drive to the top of Signal

Easily the most energizing, entertaining, and rewarding walks in the City of St. John's are the ones that take you to the top of Signal Hill National Historic Site. Whether by the main road or through the Battery neighbourhood and its adjacent trails, the payoff is the commanding vista of the mouth of St. John's Harbour and the wide open North Atlantic Ocean.

Hill, while the more hardy walk the paved road from downtown St. John's to the top, where Cabot Tower serves as the focal point of this National Historic Site of Canada. The truly adventurous take the ninety-minute North Head Trail, a hike that begins by crossing the front porch of a private home on the Outer Battery Road. One segment of the trail is a narrow rock walkway where chains are embedded into the cliff's face to help reassure, with a sure grip, the faint of heart. No matter how you get there,

the top of Signal Hill affords a commanding view of the intimate, bustling shipping harbour of St. John's, of the open ocean, and of the expanse of the city's downtown. It is not unusual to see icebergs or whales from this vantage point, as well as the World War II gun placements installed to fend off German naval forces and that now serve as tangible reminders of the role St. John's played as a military town over the centuries. Geology, military history, and human invention aside, the top of Signal Hill is also a romantic place to be, especially at night, when the stars light the sky and the waves echo up the escarpment as they crash on the rocks below.

Jelly Bean Row

Stroll along Jelly Bean Row and you know you couldn't possibly be anyplace in Canada other than downtown St. John's. The term refers to the clusters of three-storey Victorian-style buildings characterized by merrily coloured facades, highly individualized front doors, and distinctive white window casements and fascias. They cascade in sequence down the city's hilled streets in humble echoes of San Francisco. Several downtown streets offer some of these delightful architectural surprises, but they were originally most noticeable in an area called the Battery, a mish-mash of buildings, some of which cling perilously to rock cliffs over St. John's Harbour. "Jelly Bean Row" used to be a derogatory term for rows of poorer downtown houses where residents had made do with old marine paint

typically used on fishing boats and dories. Today, however, the shoe is on the other foot. As several of the city's downtown neighbourhoods have evolved into a heightened heritage district, anyone living along a Jelly Bean Row is now assumed to have status. Regardless, Jelly Bean Row is an urban landscape photographer's dream. Some of these joyful structures have exaggerated fronts with dormers, porches, bay windows, and flower boxes, while others are plain and simple. But fancy or ordinary, the houses of downtown St. John's evoke the colourful personalities of the "townies," people with dialects, phrases, and sayings that unmistakably identify them as Newfoundlanders

Imagine a colour and you will find it gracing the façade of a house somewhere in downtown St. John's, where the buildings are as full of character as the people who live there.

L'Anse aux Meadows

Christopher Columbus's fame shows that he and Queen Isabella of Spain had a more effective public relations strategy, but the fact is the Vikings were here first. In fact, the Vikings arrived in the New World nearly five hundred years before Columbus, around 1000 A.D. It has been substantiated that it was the Norse who had first contact with North American native peoples (and they had been in North America for at least five thousand years). L'Anse aux Meadows National Historic Site, at the northwestern tip of Newfoundland, pays homage to these important aspects of North American history

The best phrase to describe the significance of L'Anse aux Meadows is "pre-contact." It has been verified that the Vikings were in what became known as North America more than five hundred years before Columbus first encountered the continent's native peoples.

using clear archaeological and paleo-ecological evidence to support the hypothesis that the Vikings were the first Europeans in North America. For example, L'Anse aux Meadows is the first place where iron is known to have been smelted in North America, a discovery made in the early 1960s by Norwegian explorer and writer Helge Ingstad and his wife, Anne Stine Ingstad. They found overgrown bumps and ridges that looked like the remnants of sod houses scattered across the terrain near L'Anse aux Meadows. Over a number of years, the Ingstads and their archaeological teams went on to discover eight Norse buildings of the same kind as those used in Iceland and Greenland around the year 1000. The buildings have since been reconstructed as archivists and curators envision what life was like for the first Norse visitors to North America. The experience is augmented by site animators and a large interpretation centre enriched with artifacts gleaned from the Ingstad digs. To stand where the Vikings stood and witness how they lived is inspiring. To think that they ventured from Europe in their primitive vessels to lands unknown is nothing short of astonishing.

Cape Spear Lighthouse

If not for the curvature of the earth, you'd be able to see the coast of England from Cape Spear. The Cape Spear Lighthouse, just minutes from the capital of St. John's, is the most easterly point in North America. It also just happens to be the oldest surviving lighthouse in all of Newfoundland and Labrador, first put into operation in 1836. The first lighthouse, now gone, was built not far away, at Fort Amherst at the narrow entrance to St. John's Harbour. For decades Cape Spear has served as a guiding light for mariners, a light necessitated by the frequent fog and rocky shores near the easterly approach to the city harbour. Part of Cape Spear's history includes its role as a lookout for spotting World War Two U-boats and raiders that posed a real threat to convoys moving between Europe and North America (St. John's was often a stopover). Fortifications built at the site included soldiers' barracks and underground tunnels for their safe passage, most of which were closed or demolished after the cessation of hostilities in 1945. But the remnants of the ten-inch guns that protected the site still stand as a sobering reminder of just how close the war actually came to home along the Atlantic Canada coast. Today, except for the roar of the surf against the craggy shoreline, things are much more peaceful; the only invaders are the pods of humpback, minke, and fin whales that are easily spotted from the heights of Cape Spear, just as they are from across St. John's Harbour at towering Signal Hill.

Even if the interpretation panels didn't tell you so, Cape Spear Lighthouse certainly creates the sensation that you are standing at the easternmost edge of North America.

Newfoundland and Labrador place names run the gamut when it comes to funny and unusual, everything from Dildo to Come-by-Chance to Nick's Nose Cove. Witless Bay is among those dozens of names that visitors find so amusing and locals talk of with immense pride. As is usually the case, there is a legitimate reason for the town's name. This story goes that Captain Whittle and his family from Dorsetshire, England, were among those to first settle on the bay, less than half an hour from St. John's on the Irish Loop scenic drive. Hence Whittles Bay. But when the captain died and his wife and family returned to England, the name was colloquially altered to Whittle-less Bay.

Over time, the name evolved. Part of what makes the area special today is its designation as the Witless Bay Ecological Reserve, comprised of Gull, Green, Great, and Pee Pee islands, home of the province's largest Atlantic puffin colony, estimated to congregate here to the tune of 260,000 pairs (the puffin is the province's official bird). The reserve also gives haven to the second-largest Leach's storm-petrel colony in the world—an astonishing 620,000 nesting pairs. The list goes on to include black-legged kittiwakes and common murres, which also appear in the thousands. All of these species nest here between April and September. Access to the colonies is restricted and, except by

The Witless Bay Ecological Reserve is for the birds, literally, including the species which most captures the imagination of visitors, the toucan-like Atlantic puffin.

special research permit, is controlled by licensed marine excursion operators, who are able to sail within metres of the habitat. The Canadian Wildlife Service and Memorial University of Newfoundland have been carrying out extensive research programs in the Witless Bay Ecological Reserve for years. Their studies of the birds' behaviour and population trends, as well as the area's ecology, help guide the management of all of Newfoundland and Labrador's seabird reserves.

Cape Bonavista Lighthouse

Like so many other incredible places in Newfoundland and Labrador, Cape Bonavista is wild—waves smash ashore and birds defy gravity as they soar past grey, jagged cliffs. Nature can be such an outrageous spectacle and no place in Atlantic Canada is it more so than at Cape Bonavista. This is the place where it is believed explorer Giovanni (John) Cabot first sighted the land of the New World on June 24, 1497. Commemorated at the site in the form of a statue, Cabot would have ventured around the cape without the benefit of navigational aids. In fact it would be 346 years before a lighthouse would first be erected at the site, one of the more unusual-looking ones in all of Atlantic Canada. The navigational functions of the Cape Bonavista Lighthouse were assumed by a more modern steel tower in 1966, and the original building is now a Newfoundland Provincial Historic Museum. One of the fascinating things about the Bonavista light is that it operated with a series of hand-me-downs. The original 1843 lighting apparatus was a revolving red and white light that came from the Inchcape (Bell) Rock Lighthouse in Scotland, where it had been in use since 1811. In 1895 it in turn was replaced by the apparatus from Newfoundland's Harbour Grace Island Lighthouse, which originally came from the Isle of May, Scotland. The Cape Bonavista Lighthouse property is a great place to explore, as is the nearby town of Bonavista, a town increasingly more developed for tourism. The Ryan Premises provide a healthy dollop of historical information and displays, but perhaps the town's most interesting feature is the nearby docked replica of the *Matthew*, a sixty-five-foot caravel-style vessel built and launched in 1997 to re-enact Cabot's accomplishments as part of the five-hundred-year anniversary of his arrival in North America.

Amongst the hundreds of lighthouses still standing in Atlantic Canada, none is more colourful, with its distinctive red and white markings, than the one at Cape Bonavista on Newfoundland and Labrador's east coast.

R efugees from the white glaciers of western Greenland, icebergs are no longer going to waste as they pass through Iceberg Alley, the marine channel that begins near the northern tip of Labrador and continues down the eastern coast of Newfoundland. While icebergs have always been a fascination in Newfoundland and Labrador—purported to be the best and most reliable place in the world to see these monuments of frozen time—human enterprise has found a sustainable way to bring their byproduct to a refrigerator near you. Scientists tell us more than 90 percent of an iceberg

There are few if any guarantees in life, but one of the closest is the odds of seeing one of nature's ocean wonders in Iceberg Alley, the nickname given to the body of water stretching from the northern tip of Labrador to the east coast of Newfoundland.

is below the ocean's surface, but the 10 percent we can see turns out to be prime for harvesting. Main Brook Waterworks, established in Main Brook, just off the Viking Trail in northwestern Newfoundland, has done the obvious: harvesting water by chipping away at passing icebergs and then bottling it.

By using 100 percent biodegradable, reusable, and recyclable glass, the company claims that its product can be considered completely carbon neutral.

As for realizing your own iceberg experience, most encounters are unpredictable and can occur

anyplace on the west, north, and east coasts of the province. But the odds are greater while touring the west coast by car along the Viking Trail overlooking Iceberg Alley (aka the Labrador Straits). Or you can jump aboard the vessels of any number of charter operators throughout the province who specialize in iceberg sightings. Or, your can simply relax on the front lawn of the gracious and remote Tickle Inn at Cape Onion, Newfoundland. Here you can toast cousins of the icebergs you are sipping on as they float gently by, knowing you are doing your part for sustainability.

Once a thriving, vital fishing station serving several European nations, the Labrador Sea island of Battle Harbour is now a remote heritage travel destination that is accessible only by marine charter.

On the approach into Battle Harbour via the passenger ferry that sails to and from Mary's Harbour at the northern end of the Labrador Coastal Drive, visitors' eyes are tricked by the still forms of workers staring out from the island's wooden docks. In the right light, these life-sized photographic cutouts are amazingly realistic. Like everything else about Battle Island and its harbour, the figures contribute to a powerful sense of place; that they welcome you in silence contributes to the

island's sense of peace and solitude. The volunteer-led Battle Harbour Historic Trust is responsible for enlivening a place that for two centuries was the economic and social centre of the southeastern Labrador Coast, at one time the unofficial capital of Labrador, thanks to the island's close proximity to the cod and seal fisheries of the Labrador Sea. First established by the English as a saltfish mercantile operation in the mid-1700s, Battle Harbour developed into a vital community before

its importance waned as economies and settlement trends changed. The Historic Trust breathed new life into the remnant buildings and surrounding lands, commemorating the hard but rewarding lives of the fishermen and mercantile employees and their families. Battle Harbour is not a convenient destination, but in Newfoundland and Labrador, the most intriguing places seldom are. The area's significance goes well beyond the fishery: before Europeans arrived in the New World, aboriginal people, including Palaeoeskimo, recent Inuit, and Innu, called this island and other parts of Labrador their home; the Royal National Mission to Deep Sea Fishermen, under Dr. Wilfred Grenfell, established a hospital in the community in 1892; Marconi set up wireless operations there; and using the Marconi setup, Commander Robert E. Peary famously held two wireless press conferences from Battle Harbour to announce to the world that he'd reached the North Pole, touching off the great controversy between Peary and Frederick Cook as to who'd ventured there first. The trust operates accommodations in the homes and cottages (including that of the revered Dr. Grenfell himself) that have been repatriated and restored, as well as food service and interactive interpretation, making Battle Harbour a cherished respite from whatever happens to be going on in the rest of the world.

Red Bay Whaling Station

Occupied originally by Basques fishermen in the early sixteenth century, Red Bay and the whale oil harvested there is said to have kept Europe alight for one hundred years. Many of the artifacts at this fascinating national historic site were discovered through underwater archaeology.

Traditional archaeology is, under the best of conditions, a lengthy and painstaking endeavour. Imagine, then, scouring for the history of human culture within the cold, shifting waters of the North Atlantic's Strait of Belle Isle. In 1978, a team of underwater archaeologists, led by Parks Canada's Robert Grenier, unearthed a treasure trove of sunken ships and artifacts, tangible remnants from a sixteenth-century colony of Basques fishermen who harvested and processed the oil from so many right and bowhead whales that it's said they lit Europe for a hundred years. The Basques had expanded their base of operation after exhausting the stocks in their own Bay of Biscay, the result of centuries of overfishing. The industry they established in the New World, despite being

thousands of kilometres away, created sizable profits for the men who sponsored it. At the time of Grenier's first excursions, the discipline of underwater archaeology was hardly a tried-and-true technique. But dig and sift they did, with precision and ingenuity, until the underpinnings of the Red Bay story clearly emerged. When combined with documents in Europe and traditional land-based archaeology at Red Bay, researchers proved the hypothesis that the Basques had visited and worked in the region for decades. A number of the visiting men never made their way home; a whalers' cemetery on Saddle Island in Red Bay Harbour houses more than 60 graves, containing about 140 skeletons. According to experts, the burial of more than one individual in a single grave likely indicates

concurrent accidental deaths due to drowning or exposure, both of which were continuous hazards for the Basque whalers. In 2000, Parks Canada officially opened the Red Bay National Historic Site and interpretation centre, commemorating the Basques' industriousness at an estimated sixteen harbour working stations along the Quebec and Labrador coasts. This site is one of the precious destinations that help explain the rising popularity of the Labrador Coastal Drive.

A special, spiritual place in the hearts and minds of many Labrador Inuit, the Moravian Mission at Hebron was established in 1831 and once served as the northernmost settlement in all of Labrador.

There are many stories emanating from the nineteenth-century Moravian Mission at Hebron, in northern Labrador, but none more stirring and disturbing than that involving an Inuit man, Abraham Ulrikab, and his family. Ulrikab was a devout Christian who had been schooled by Moravian missionaries. Yet in 1880, he and his family were shamefully transported to Europe, where they were exhibited in zoos, only to contract smallpox and die. It was one of several episodes that demonstrated how people from outside Hebron had little understanding of the community's people and their culture. In 1959, the Canadian government relocated those remaining at Hebron, numbering just fifty-nine families following several epidemics, including the influenza pandemic of

1918, to larger communities within the Labrador territory (now called Nunatsiavut). The mission was to be forever closed. For most of those who were relocated, the transition was disastrous: the Hebron residents, out of their natural element of fishing and hunting, suffered from poverty and a lack of belonging. It took fifty years before the Government of Newfoundland and Labrador offered an official apology to the former residents of Hebron for what had occurred. Today the mission is undergoing a painstaking stabilization, preservation, and restoration effort, decades after being secured and declared a national historic site by Parks Canada in 1979. Its distinctive design seems oddly familiarity to the Hebron landscape. Built in Germany, disassembled, and then reconstructed at the Labrador site, the mission's main structure is what makes Hebron visually more recognizable than any other tract of land in the north. Today, the site is a place of emotional connection for those remaining Inuit who were relocated in 1959, as it is for their descendants. In spite of its remoteness, Hebron is also becoming popular as a landing site for cruise ship tourists who have an affinity for northern travel and who are intrigued by the mysteries of the Labrador Inuit.

Torngat Mountains National Park Fjords

Words cannot describe the sensation of being within one of Canada's newest national parks, the Torngat Mountains National Park in Northern Labrador. The mountains, in particular, have a spiritual grip on the region's aboriginal people, the Labrador Inuit.

Canada's newest national park is one of the world's oldest places. The Torngat Mountains National Park, situated at the northern extremity of the Labrador coast, form a range of high barren mountains where the more southerly Labrador Inuit say their spirit, Torngarsoak, resides. For the people of newly named Nunatsiavut, the territory that now encompasses several Inuit communities as well as the national park, the legend of Torngarsoak and the majesty of the massive coastal fjords are perpetual. The Torngats are a wild place, where polar bears, wolves, and caribou survive in a habitat that is breathtakingly spectacular, physically daunting, and it turns out, militarily strategic: Saglek Bay at the southern edge of the park has served as a joint Canadian-U.S. defence northern warning station. Since the Cold War, it has been one of a string of Arctic and Subarctic installations that

formed part of what was once known as the Dew Line. The Torngats are a dichotomy of large-scale, eye-piercing mountaintop lakes, tiny, delicate flora such as mountain cranberries and Arctic poppies, and rock formations once described by geologist Oscar M. Lieber as "revel(ing) in their freedom." In fact, experts claim that the age characteristics of the Torngats factor in 80 percent of the earth's entire geologic history. There are only two places in the world exhibiting rock formations older than those found here: the Northwest Territories and Australia. Working in association with the newly formed Tourism Nunatsiavut and Parks Canada, cruise ship and land adventure operators have begun to trickle into the area under controlled circumstances that help to ensure the integrity of the land and the ocean, the two elements forming the lifeblood of the Labrador Inuit.

Sir Richard Squires
Memorial Provincial Park

From the viewing platforms overlooking Big Falls at Sir Richard Squires Memorial Provincial Park on Newfoundland's Humber River, you'd swear you were inside a National Geographic documentary film. The platforms provide a perfect place to watch the astonishing and inspiring leaping of Atlantic salmon up the wall of rock and water as they continue their upstream spawning migration from the Atlantic Ocean to the place of their birth. The salmon make attempt after attempt against the power and rush of the Humber's current and the height of its most noteworthy natural waterfall. The provincial park commemorates two-time Newfoundland prime minister Richard Squires (1919–1923 and 1928–1932), who served just before the province joined the Dominion of Canada in 1949. Although the park offers whitewater canoeing, camping, and hiking, it is most renowned for its salmon fishing. Newfoundlanders and non-residents who frequented the area tended to covet what they considered to be the most prized pools, spots with names such as Piercy's Hole, Goosney's Rock, and Wendy's Pool, to name a few. Just over half an hour from the western Newfoundland community of Deer Lake, there is no doubting that the site of the Big Falls, especially concurrent with the spawning activity of the salmon, is well worth the drive. On a sunny day, it is the most ideal of places to enjoy a picnic lunch while watching the lonely but happy anglers silently whip their lines across the Humber's glistening surface.

The sight of migrating salmon leaping against the force of the Big Falls of the Humber River at Sir Richard Squires Provincial Park is one of the most awesome natural spectacles in Atlantic Canada.

Nova Scotia

LEGEND
1. Tidal Bore Rafting on the Shubenacadie River
2. Crown Jewel Resort Dogsledding
3. Halifax Heritage District Pub
4. Peggy's Cove
5. Stan Rogers Canso Folk Festival
6. Maritime Museum of the Atlantic
7. The Ovens
8. Grand Pré National Historic Site
9. Keltic Lodge Resort and the
    Highlands Links Golf Course
10. Historic Lunenburg
11. The Halifax Citadel
12. Halifax's Historic Properties
13. Seaside Adjunct—Kejimkujik
    National Park
14. Balancing Rock
15. Kayaking at Cape Chignecto
16. Cape d'Or Lighthouse

17. Joggins
18. Nova Scotia Wild
    Blueberry Festival
19. Rita MacNeil's Tea Room
20. Fortress of Louisbourg
21. Antigonish Highland Games
22. Glace Bay Miners' Museum
23. Restaurant Chez Christophe
24. Annapolis Valley Wine Tour
25. Canada's Inland Sea—the Bras d'or Lakes
26. Glenora Distillery
27. Sugar Moon Maple Farm
28. Cycling the Cabot Trail
29. St. Ann's Gaelic College
30. Bird Islands, Englishtown
31. Skyline Trail
32. Cape Forchu Light Station
33. Kenomee Canyon Trail System
34. Apple Blossom Festival
35. Surfing at Lawrencetown

Tidal Bore Rafting on the Shubenacadie River

It begins with a lazy, strategically timed ride past the sandbars and mudflats of Nova Scotia's largest river, the Shubenacadie. Soon there is a modest ripple, a subtle hint that the Bay of Fundy's low tidal cycle has done its about-face, and the sense of expectation rises. Then there is a second ripple, slightly less subtle, and so it begins to build. The tidal bore raft, really a modern Zodiac, carrying eight passengers and a guide who controls an outboard motor, barely bobs. But within seconds, one of the

Tidal bore rafting has been compared to being in the agitator cycle of a washing machine. The difference is passengers don't come out clean, although they do come out happy.

world's most amazing marine phenomena—the Fundy tidal bore—is in full-fledged action mode, and the passengers are holding on for dear life. For the next half an hour, the Zodiac will turn and spin as though inside the agitator of a giant washing machine, the cold brown water of the Fundy's tributaries soaking everything aboard in spite of the operator-supplied life jacket, rain gear, and rubber boots. The intensity of the experience changes with the position of the moon and the playfulness of the rafting guides, who are experts at extracting the most excitement out of every "tidal wave." Compared to traditional whitewater rafting experiences that deliver an intermittent sequence of intense thrills over several hours, tidal bore rafting is a seamless, uninterrupted thrill-ride from the moment the bore intensifies. The trip is always followed by a celebration of high-fives and raucous laughter, not to mention the typical post-adventure hot shower and barbecue, which are nearly as gratifying as the rafting itself.

Crown Jewel Resort Dogsledding

The stereotype of dogsledding is banished with one visit to the Crown Jewel Resort near Baddeck on Cape Breton Island. Being a musher in the twenty-first century involves more than just standing at the back of a sled and yelling commands to a team of dogs. At Crown Jewel, qualified instructors lead visitors into their comfort zone with what might seem like a pack of howling wolves, but are really the indigenous species of the trusted husky dogs used in Canada's north. The Crown Jewel experience is for most a once-in-a-lifetime experience. It is also a confidence-building excursion that not only introduces visitors to the art of sledding, but also to "skijoring" (cross-country skiing while being harnessed to dogs with a bungee cord) and, in the off-season, "dog-scootering"

(done on modified rubber-tire, flat-terrain scooters pulled by the dogs). Sledding experimenters can try a half-day excursion while the more adventurous can book multi-day lodge-to-lodge trips sure to test winter hardiness. But this is much more than a thrill ride; the experience is set against the backdrop of magnificent rural Cape Breton and operated by owners who espouse the practices of an eco-destination that is environmentally sensitive, sustainable, educational, and that features organically grown vegetables, organically raised livestock, and resort facilities constructed with reclaimed timber frames and the latest in low-impact energy and water usage. No one ever said fun and outdoor adventure could not be sustainable.

For bragging rights to something friends or neighbours probably haven't done, a dogsledding adventure at Crown Jewel Resort is certainly worth adding to your list.

Downtown Halifax's Historic Properties form an ideal backdrop for a traditional-style Irish pub where the draft beer and the music are every bit as authentic as anything you're likely to find in Dublin.

Halifax's Old Triangle Irish Alehouse stands for more than just draft beer, pub food, and musical gatherings known as "sessions." It is a very able representative for the cluster of establishments found primarily in the city's well-preserved heritage zone and helps explain why pubbing in Halifax seems like such a robust and authentic experience. The triangle in the name represents a number of symbolic Irish images. The alehouse's emblem is a Celtic knot, which harkens back to the shamrock and the triple spirals of the large prehistoric Irish tomb and fairy mound known as Newgrange. The pub's name loosely refers to the fact it was created by three Irishmen, and that it contains three areas known as the Snug, the Pourhouse, and Tigh An Cheoil (a house of music). The name has also been said to suggest the activities of singing, talking, and merriment (in Gaelic, Ceol, Caint Agus Craic), taken from the song "The Auld Triangle," which is featured in the play, *The Quare Fellow* by Irishman Brendan Behan (who once famously described himself as "a drinker with a writing problem"). The triangle in the song's title refers to the large metal triangle that was beaten daily in Mountjoy Prison to waken the inmates (Behan was once incarcerated there).

Found in the thick of Halifax's historic district, the building housing the Old Triangle was once the home of Nova Scotia premier and lieutenant governor Joseph Howe, a double irony in that he was a strong promoter of temperance who also became embroiled in controversies between his ruling protestant class and the city's Irish Catholics, a debate so nasty that it cost him an election.

The Old Triangle is not unique in keeping Haligonians and visitors refreshed: the city is purported to have more bars and pubs per capita

than anyplace else in North America. Although the Old Triangle is arguably at the epicentre of the city's nightlife, it takes only a minute or two to walk to any of the downtown area's other pubs—longstanding icons like The Split Crow, The Henry House, O'Carroll's, and The Lower Deck. These, too, are hearty party places offering a modern version of the traditional pub experience that sailors and townspeople in Halifax have enjoyed for more than two hundred years.

Peggy's Cove, one of the most visited and photographed sites in the entire nation, is nearly as iconic as the maple leaf or the beaver.

The tiny village is so widely exposed in travel literature and tour operator itineraries that even visitors from abroad have a sense of expectation about the place long before arriving. The Peggy's Cove lighthouse is a classic, with its white column, red tower, and beaming light standing vigilant over an unmistakable outcrop of grey granite that always tempts visitors to flirt with the wild and dangerous ebb and flow of the Atlantic Ocean. To many, this community is representative of the idyllic Atlantic fishing village, a notion stretched to the limits by the constant line of buses, RVs, and cars that deposit people in the parking lot adjacent to the point's natural offerings. The Peggy's Cove Commission Act of 1961 attempted to rein in development, but it seems there is no stopping fascination with the site. This makes winter, spring, and fall some of the best times of year to visit, when Peggy's Cove's natural wonders can be more exclusively yours to enjoy and contemplate. The public's fascination with Peggy's Cove grew all the more after the 1998 crash of Swissair Flight 111 just offshore from the community, tragically claiming 229 lives. A nearby memorial recalls the powerful sense of community and the tradition of "neighbours helping neighbours" that emerged as locals set off in their fishing boats that night to search for survivors and, in the aftermath, welcomed and comforted victims' family members from around the world. This wasn't the first memorial to be erected at or near Peggy's Cove. Visitors can't help but notice the large granite carving by Finnish sculptor William E. DeGarthe (who once lived in the community) depicting thirty-two fishermen and their wives and children, all protected by the wings of a guardian angel. It evokes both the dangers of the sea and the closeness of the people here who—like in other Maritime villages— come together as one in times of disasters big and small.

Peggy's Cove is so endearing and enduring that it transcends its own cliché as the stereotypical picture postcard destination in Nova Scotia.

Stan Rogers Folk Festival

Most people assume that because of the regional flavour, authenticity, and richness of the late musician Stan Rogers's compositions, that he was born and bred someplace in Atlantic Canada. In fact, he grew up in Dundas, Ontario, the son of Maritimers who'd followed the work exodus to Central Canada in the late 1940s. Rogers developed his appreciation for Maritime music during his summers visiting Guysborough, Nova Scotia. And Rogers's legacy carries on long after his tragic death in an airplane fire at just thirty-three years of age in 1983.

Known colloquially as "Stanfest," the festival cast in his name and honour is staged each July in the town of Canso, near the strait that separates Cape Breton from the Nova Scotia mainland. The three-day festival has grown in scale and international stature over the years, attracting names such as Don McLean (of "American Pie" fame) and legendary folk artist Pete Seeger. With Canso hungry for an infusion of optimism (the community's historic fishing industry virtually collapsed in the 1990s), Stanfest has served as a welcome annual affair, quadrupling the local population for a few days as the music and voices of artists echo across the waves of the Atlantic Ocean. The ten-thousand-plus visitors overflow traditional accommodations into RV and tent cities where impromptu musical gatherings are every bit as entertaining, involving, and memorable as the programmed events which take place on the festival's main stages.

The Stan Rogers Folk Festival has gone way beyond folksy and is now regarded as one of the premier musical festivals in North America, both by leading artists and their fans.

Maritime Museum of the Atlantic

The Maritime Museum of the Atlantic's *Titanic* exhibit attracts an international audience. The in-depth interpretation and range of artifacts make the museum a must-see stop on Halifax's bustling waterfront.

Maritime museums are nearly as common in maritime zones as lighthouses, with many communities taking pride in their connections to ships and the sea. But as one of the prized jewels of the Nova Scotia museum network, Halifax's Maritime Museum of the Atlantic takes the concept up several notches. With exhibitions overseen by world-calibre curators, the Maritime Museum plans and designs exhibits that illustrate and demonstrate countless fascinating facts and stories about humankind's connections to the sea. The museum's vast collections emphasize the marine history of Nova Scotia, but expand to cover the Royal Navy, Royal Canadian Navy, Canadian merchant marine, and even Nova Scotia shipwrecks and their treasures. The most popular exhibits and stories are those focussing on the Halifax Explosion of 1917, the sinking of the *Titanic*, and the North Atlantic convoy's struggle against German U-boats during World War Two. Overlooking eastern Canada's most happening harbour and within a heartbeat of Halifax's popular Historic Properties, the museum could not be more perfectly situated.

The Ovens

More than 150 years ago, they came for the gold, but today they come to the Ovens for its natural beauty. In the possession of the Chapin family—yes, of the same extraction as musician Harry Chapin—the Ovens' 190 acres of coastal forest and sea caves near the community of Riverport, Nova Scotia, is a rare and extraordinary parcel of privately owned ocean frontage. Once owned by the Cunards of the famous Cunard Shipping Line, the Ovens was the site of an 1861 gold rush that saw a thousand people descend on the property. With its gold mining stories, beaches, and caves that have names like Tucker's Tunnel, Indian Cave, and Cannon Cave, the Ovens is a perfect exploration for families.

The Chapins run a campground on the property and family members can be regularly found singing and playing their instruments in the Ol' Gold Miner Diner, at impromptu campfires, and most especially during their Chapin Family Concert by the Sea Weekend, staged annually in mid-August. Those still believing there may be gold on Cunard Beach can rent a pan and learn the techniques of panning the very way the old prospectors did. The real gold, however, is there for everyone: the thrill of exploring the caves of the Ovens and savouring the site's outstanding views of Lunenburg Harbour and a series of nearby islands.

Although made famous for its association with nineteenth-century gold discoveries, contemporary interest in The Ovens is focused on the highly accessible cave formations and beaches which surround the park.

Grand Pré National Historic Site

Designated by Parks Canada as a national historic site in 1961, Grand Pré commemorates the French Acadians from the time of their initial settlement in northeastern North America in 1682, to their infamous deportation from the region in the mid-eighteenth century, to their more recent cultural revival. The grounds at Grand Pré include an interpretive exhibit, multimedia theatre, and gift shop, but more importantly, the site is a peaceful, secluded refuge—a place of contemplation for people from around the world linked through their Acadian ancestry (as well as for those who aren't).

Few attractions evoke the same level of emotion as Grand Pré National Historic Site, the Annapolis Valley destination commemorating the story of the Acadians.

The lawns and walkways are adorned with gardens and towering trees, including a cluster of four-hundred-year-old French willows, with trunks as thick and craggy as ancient forests, and branches that gnarl and twist as though conjured up by an angry god. Beyond the boundaries of the historic site exists a wealth of more tangible evidence of the Acadians' early presence in the Annapolis Valley: a complex system of dykes engineered by these industrious French settlers. Found along the shores of the Bay of Fundy's beautiful Minas Basin, the dykes set the original stage for the valley becoming the agricultural heartland of Nova Scotia.

The centrepiece of the Grand Pré site itself is the sculpted memorial to the epic poem,

Évangeline: A Tale of Acadie, written by Henry Wadsworth Longfellow in 1847. The story of a young Acadian girl and the heart-wrenching search for her lost love, Gabriel, *Évangeline* is so universal in its appeal that it has been popularized in at least three feature film adaptations dating from as early as 1913. It is against the backdrop of this elegantly sculpted figure that Grand Pré emerges as a peaceful, secluded refuge and wonderful place of contemplation for all visitors, but especially for people from around the world who share Acadian ancestry.

"Natural artistry" is the phrase used to describe the late, legendary architect Stanley Thompson's design philosophy for the Highlands Links Golf Course and other destination courses he created during his career.

Natural and human design come together at the Keltic Lodge Resort and the Highlands Links Golf Course at Ingonish, Cape Breton. The lodge, one of three Nova Scotia government-sponsored "signature resorts," has the classic lines of an Old World resort property and is graced on three sides by the Atlantic Ocean. The golf course, meanwhile, has the unmistakable traits of a Stanley Thompson design. This is apparent even though Parks Canada has updated the course by combining its own sustainability practices with those of the Audubon Cooperative Sanctuary System of Canada in certifying the Highlands Links as a Cooperative Sanctuary site. This notion of the Highland Links being maintained in a natural state is completely in keeping with Thompson's own vision. As the creator of some of the world's finest golf experiences,

the late golf course architect was famous for his philosophy of "natural artistry": moulding and shaping topography in ways that complemented the natural features of the land. Thompson had the uncanny ability to combine breathtaking views with golf holes that looked like they were meant to be there. Working with the magnificence of the Cape Breton Highlands, Thompson must have thought he was in heaven. He was hired by the then-National Park Service in 1939 to create a nine-hole course in the heart of the Highlands. Halfway through the project, however, Thompson convinced his clients that an eighteen-hole course was essential to do the site justice. Thompson looked to Cape Breton and Scottish heritage in christening each of the Highlands Links' holes with a Scottish name, including "Caber's Toss," "Bonnie Burn," and the Gaelic "Heich O' Fash," which translates as "the height of trouble." Any golfer, no matter how avid, would be wise to play at least one round on the links at the Cape Breton Highlands.

Historic Lunenburg

For generations, Lunenburg has rung synonymous with the *Bluenose*, the world-famous vessel renowned as the undefeated champion of the North Atlantic fishing fleet and of several international schooner races. Built in and launched from this South Shore town in 1921, the schooner was sadly lost off a Haitian reef in 1946. It was replicated in 1963 by the *Bluenose II*, which was crafted in the same shipyard and by many of the same men as the original. But Lunenburg's association to this important Canadian icon (the Canadian ten-cent coin has carried the proud *Bluenose* image for decades), has nearly been surpassed by the town's 1995 designation as a UNESCO World Heritage Site. "Old Town Lunenburg," as the designation is phrased, received recognition as the best remaining example of a planned British colonial settlement in

North America. There is no better way to explain the town's significance than to quote directly from UNESCO's own inscription: "Old Town Lunenburg is a well preserved example of 18th century British colonial urban planning, which has undergone no significant changes since its foundation and which largely continues to fulfill the economic and social purposes for which it was designed. Of special importance is its diversified and well-preserved vernacular architectural tradition, which spans over 250 years…It is an excellent example of an urban community and culture designed for and based on the offshore Atlantic fishery which is undergoing irreversible change and is evolving in a form that cannot yet be fully defined." A stroll through the town gives visitors an up-close perspective on these recognitions, especially the way in which modern-

Sea captains' homes and fishing warehouses shape the waterfront of the south shore town of Lunenburg, earning it a UNESCO designation as a World Heritage Site.

day residents and businesspeople have integrated their lives with the past, the cornerstones being the continued use of the historic waterfront and the retention of its priceless architecture. A true icon along southern Nova Scotia's prized Lighthouse Route, Lunenburg still possesses a tangible sense of time and place that few if any communities on the Eastern Seaboard have managed to retain.

The Halifax Citadel

When the Halifax Citadel clock strikes noon, there is a coinciding cannon blast that pierces through the din of traffic in the city's downtown. If you're a city resident, the crackle and boom of the official noon-day gun strike a reassuring chord of familiarity; if you're visiting and unaware of the explosion's source, it can be downright jarring, if not alarming. The firing of the nearby gun has been a tradition since the British had their first presence in the area in 1749. The more innocent clock is the centrepiece of the most prevalent landmark in all of Halifax—the Halifax Citadel fortress, the crowning achievement of what was designed as a multi-faceted Halifax Defense

Complex, a series of military facilities still found in the strategic port city. The Citadel fortress has been restored to the mid-Victorian period and is operated by Parks Canada as a national historic site, providing the visitor interaction and spectacle of the kilted 78th Highland Regiment, the Royal Artillery, and other animators representing figures from the fortress's early days. The Citadel is one of the most prominent fortifications in any city in North America, and from its founding in 1749 through the nineteenth century, was one of four principal overseas naval stations in the British Empire. The present Citadel was completed in 1856, a massive star-shaped bastion fortification surrounded by

The most prominent historic British fortress in Atlantic Canada, the Halifax Citadel is the centrepiece in a city whose very existence is predicated on things military.

a defence ditch, ramparts, a musketry gallery, a powder magazine, and signal masts. Under Parks Canada's stewardship, it is also rich with stories, interpretation, and demonstrations featuring the Highlanders and Royal Artillery. The blasting of the noon-day gun serves as a sharp reminder that in its earlier role as an active fortress, cannons could reach intruders in Halifax Harbour, thereby protecting the British fleet and the settlement which evolved to become, by far, the largest city in Atlantic Canada.

Halifax's Historic Properties

Although surrounded by modern office towers, the comings and goings of modern ocean-going vessels, and a large infusion of commercial activity, Halifax's Historic Properties maintain a sense of authenticity which dignifies the city's bustling waterfront.

The sheer concentration of national historic sites at Halifax's Historic Properties—seven in total—says it all: this is the most important and concentrated place of seafaring heritage and history in Canada. Standing durable and dignified on four acres of waterfront property, the Historic Properties is where seafarers began building the highly strategic port city after it was established in 1749 by Sir Edward Cornwallis, a surname that pops up repeatedly around Halifax. Because Halifax was established during the age of sail, seamen built carpenter shops and sail lofts here, and they soon needed warehouses for storing their goods. The properties became the city's central marketplace, where general merchants, grocers, insurers, and commodities dealers grew and prospered. Unbelievably, the properties were destined for demolition in the 1960s to make way for urban renewal until a group of naysayers stepped in and won the day. The result is one of the best examples of how heritage and commercialism can be intertwined. Historic Properties is brimming with offices, galleries, shops, pubs, and patio restaurants with a view of Halifax Harbour that visitors clamour for. The most obvious and best known of the buildings is Privateers Warehouse, built for captains who were licensed by the British Crown to plunder ships from enemy nations. Many

of these men worked for Enos Collins, a merchant, ship owner, banker, and privateer who at his death in 1871 was purported to be the richest man in Canada. It was here at Historic Properties where he established the Halifax Banking Company, which evolved into one of Canada's enduring, chartered banking institutions, the Canadian Imperial Bank of Commerce (now branded as CIBC). The Vice Admiralty Court is where plundered goods were sold at auction. The Pickford and Black Building was the site of a ship's chandlery that obtained many of its goods by running a steamship service back and forth to the West Indies.

The Historic Properties experience today is more than just shopping, food, and entertainment; the highlight is really walking the waterfront boardwalk. You won't be alone, as this is where most of the city's residents and visitors tend to stroll and congregate, especially during events like the Halifax International Buskers Festival or for the intermittent arrival of Tall Ships from around the world.

Seaside Adjunct–Kejimkujik National Park

There's just no denying that properly pronouncing the Mi'kmaq name Kejimkujik requires some practice and familiarization; hence the more popular and widely used nickname, "Keji." This southwestern Nova Scotia destination is both a national park and a national historic site that is actually two locations: a central inland park of lakes, rivers, and forests covering 381 square kilometres in the centre of southern Nova Scotia, and an adjunct coastal wilderness park comprising 22 square kilometres, found just south of Liverpool. Wherever you tread at Keji, you are enjoying the heritage of a Mi'kmaq cultural landscape, highlighted by traditional encampment areas. In addition to the powerful sense of place associated with the Mi'kmaq people, Parks Canada defines Keji as a "biodiversity hotspot" where visitors can find rare southerly species and the greatest assortment of reptiles and amphibians in Atlantic

Canada. When it comes to birdlife, the park plays an active role in preserving habitats for five species known to be at risk in Nova Scotia, including the Canada warbler, the chimney swift, the common nighthawk, the olive-sided flycatcher, and the rusty blackbird. Perhaps most interesting is the barred owl, a species whose survival depends on the availability of cavity trees in mature hardwoods. Keji is considered to have the greatest density of barred owls in all of Canada. For some, especially families, Keji represents a wonderful introduction to accessible Atlantic Canadian wilderness. And because far too many others take Keji for granted—turning their attention instead to well-publicized places such as the Bay of Fundy—it is a treasure that is largely wide open and uncrowded, even at peak travel times

This slice of "Keji," as Kejimkujik is called locally, is situated apart from the inland section of this national park, preserving two wholly different habitats for the enjoyment of Canadians and visitors alike.

Balancing Rock

Nova Scotia's Balancing Rock is a three-dimensional demonstration of Mother Nature's ingenious sleight of hand. It stands so precariously on one end that you'd swear a breath of wind might topple it into St. Mary's Bay. The rock is just a quick ferry ride from Digby Neck to the community of Tiverton, followed by a short ride to a small hiking park. After descending the steps to the site, most people are astonished to see that the fierce ocean winds and waves have not eroded the vertical rock from its perch. Described by scientists as metamorphosed sedimentary rock from the Cambrian-Ordovician age, Balancing Rock is sometimes referred to as a "sea stack." It is a columnar basalt formation, a rock type common along much of St. Mary's Bay. Although Balancing Rock is the best-known and most extreme sea stack example in Atlantic Canada, Mother Nature has similarly amused herself in other places around the globe, including at the Brimham Rocks in North Yorkshire, England, at the Devil's Marbles Conservation Area in the Northern Territory of Australia, and throughout the desert states of California, Utah, and Arizona. Unlike most of those other balancing rocks, the Nova Scotia site has one distinction: the surface it stands on matches its own geological composition.

Perpetually defying gravity and other worldly forces, Balancing Rock makes for one of the most fun photo ops in Nova Scotia.

Kayaking at Cape Chignecto

Sailing around Cape Chignecto in the 1700s, sea captains would have seen virgin stands of tall Nova Scotia red spruce and might have imagined them as great ships' masts. Today, Cape Chignecto is Nova Scotia's largest provincial park, a destination formed of deep valleys, sheltered coves, remnant old-growth forest, and scenic views from towering cliffs. Geologically, Chignecto is an excellent representation of continental collision, volcanic occurrences, the uplifting of mountain ranges, and glacial activity. The invisible Cobequid Fault runs through the park and serves as geologists' dividing line between northern and southern Nova Scotia.

The lands at Chignecto were used for centuries by the Aboriginal Mi'kmaq, then by the French, and finally, after their expulsion, by the British.

Whether kayaking or hiking, Nova Scotia's Cape Chignecto is one of those memorable places that puts the relationship between humankind and nature into crystal clear perspective.

Evidence of all three cultures is everywhere, even in place names within the park, like Refugee Cove and French Lookout, which refer to the Acadians and their displacement from the area in 1755. European settlement and commercial development centred around the logging and shipbuilding industries followed those early sailors' initial arrival. There are mere traces of those settlements now: a few former logging roads and old stone foundations.

It is difficult to say which perspective on Chignecto is more inspiring—from the lookouts along the park's coastal hiking vantage points or from the sea on a guided kayak tour. Chignecto's

hiking experiences are very diverse—from the Red Rock Trail (classified as "easy" and less than half an hour for completion), to the McGahey Brook Canyon Trail (a "challenging" trail that takes four to six hours), to the fifty-one-kilometre Cape Chignecto Coastal Trail, described in provincial literature as a "very challenging" experience that can take up to four days to complete even for the most experienced hiker. As well, single- or multi-day sea kayaking programs allow visitors to paddle into mysterious sea caves at high tide. (Imagine kayaking at the base of 185-metre rock walls rising from the jubilation of the Bay of Fundy's world record tides!) A highlight of the on-the-water experience is the Three Sisters rock formation, the natural crown jewel of Cape Chignecto Park.

Cape d'Or Lighthouse

Atlantic Canada's best lighthouse experiences are the ones you have to work the hardest to reach. A visit to the Cape d'Or Lighthouse, forty-five kilometres from Parrsboro on the Bay of Fundy, requires leaving the main highway to drive a six-kilometre section of gravel road, followed by a good walk down to the light from the parking lot. As the Cape d'Or Light website says: "Order a drink. Breathe. You made it." And oh is it ever worth it. The lighthouse dining area has three walls of windows—fifteen in all—that bring the sea, sky, and rocky surroundings right into the room. Enjoying a glass of wine or a beer and ordering from a menu that includes traditional Nova Scotia chowder and homemade fishcakes sets the stage for the real payoff. On a clear day, Cape d'Or offers up a superb view of Cape Split and what are called "Dory Rips," the phenomenon of choppy water created by conflicting currents within the Minas Basin. For those looking to immerse themselves more fully, there is also a guest house offering four rooms. The availability of only a few rooms means that only a select few people get to experience the life-changing experience of a Cape d'Or sunset, a star-filled sky, and the potential of a gold and blue Bay of Fundy sunrise.

A glass of wine, a glorious sunset, and the drama of the crashing tides—just another average day at Cape d'Or on Nova Scotia's Bay of Fundy shore.

Joggins

The Joggins Fossil Cliffs are world-famous for their fossils from the Coal Age—so famous that the site earned a UNESCO World Natural Heritage Site designation. According to scientists, Joggins is especially significant because its world-class cache of plant and crocodile-sized amphibian fossils are accompanied by fossils of the world's oldest reptiles, actually pre-dating dinosaurs and the mammals of later ages. (Dinosaurs did not even appear on earth for another 100 million years after the Joggins fossil era.) The Joggins cliffs form a paleontological path stretching along fifteen kilometres of Bay of Fundy shoreline, reaching back 315 million years. For all that time, Joggins has been a place on the move; it was once near the Earth's equator, forming part of a massive swampy river delta that lay between the Appalachian and Atlas mountains. The UNESCO designation has significantly enhanced the community's stature and its claim to fossil fame. The designation also opens the door to special financial considerations from governments and the private sector that will aid in the community's effort to preserve and protect their prized world natural heritage resource. Built as the primary facility for the geological experience, the Joggins Fossil Centre serves as the disembarkation point for interpretive tours to the actual coastal fossil site, as well as housing facilities for scientists.

Scientists have long known that Joggins is a special place where much of the world's natural history can be calculated. Now, with its official designation by UNESCO as a World Natural Heritage Site, the rest of the world knows about Joggins too.

Nova Scotia Wild Blueberry Festival

Every berry native to Atlantic Canada is celebrated in one community or another, and the blueberry is no exception. The Nova Scotia Wild Blueberry Festival is centred in Oxford, home of the largest blueberry processor in the world.

Mention the name "Oxford" to practically anybody in Nova Scotia and the image of blueberries comes to mind. The town is home to Oxford Frozen Foods, the world's largest processor of wild blueberries (and the world's second-larger producer of blueberries, after the state of Maine). Although Oxford is the undisputed centre of the industry, the Wild Blueberry Festival is celebrated throughout central Nova Scotia, from Amherst to Parrsboro to Truro to Stewiacke. Staged in late August, the festival is a celebration of exhibitions; farmers' markets; quilt and craft fairs; bake sales; blueberry, salad, and ham suppers; concerts; pie-eating contests; and every type of blueberry dish

you could dream up: traditional blueberry pie, blueberry crisp, blueberry smoothies, blueberry chutney, blueberry wine, blueberry preserves, and traditional Mi'kmaq recipes, including those that were once used for medicinal purposes. (Speaking of medicinal, it's only in recent years that blueberries have become widely appreciated as an antioxidant.) You know the blueberry has made its way across nearly every consumer spectrum when there's word that the Nova Scotia festival now includes a Wild Blueberry Motorcycle Tour, with bikers riding through wild blueberry country with a final destination of the Wild Blueberry Teddy Bear Picnic at the Oxford Lion's Club Park.

Rita MacNeil's Tea Room

What is it about Nova Scotia women and their extraordinary musical talent? Must be something in the water, as they say. Springhill's Anne Murray, Halifax's Sarah McLachlan, and Cape Breton's Natalie MacMaster and the Rankin family all have one thing in common: small town sensibility and international stardom. Cape Breton songstress Rita MacNeil is no different, except for the fact that she is arguably the most accessible of the lot, thanks to the creation of her commercial tea room and gift shop in the Cape Breton community of Big Pond. On a monthly basis throughout the late spring, summer, and early fall, MacNeil makes a point of attending her pre-publicized "meet and greets," held while guests are dining and browsing for souvenirs in the former schoolhouse that she converted in 1986. The menu is, of course,

musically themed: "Mrs. Pott's Traditional in A Minor" is an afternoon English tea; "The Old School House Strings" features sweetbreads with preserve jams and the sinfulness of real Devonshire cream; and "The Working Man" section recalls the signature tune MacNeil performs with the haunting Men of the Deeps choir, calloused but soft-souled men from the coal mines of Cape Breton. Always on hand is MacNeil's own special blend tea. To appreciate why the creation of a cozy tea room would be important to her, one need only turn to playwright Charlie Rhindress: "MacNeil's songs are about conversations, friends getting together, community roots, believing in dreams, both good and bad times, working people, taking risks, home and paying tribute to a loving family—things that ring true for everybody."

Perennially popular Nova Scotia songstress Rita MacNeil has an immensely loyal fan following which doesn't hurt the level of traffic at the Cape Breton Island tea room which bears her name.

In terms of sheer size, the Fortress of Louisbourg is the granddaddy of national historic sites in Atlantic Canada and the largest historical reconstruction in Canada. A towering, distinctive spire rises above a sprawling complex of buildings. The French first arrived at Louisbourg in 1713 and

six years later began the construction of a fortified town that is so immense it took a quarter century to complete. There was a time when thousands resided at Louisbourg, most of them men of French, Basque, Swiss, and German origins. The settlement became known for the harvesting, drying, and salting of

Recreated with breathtaking detail, Cape Breton Island's Fortress of Louisbourg is the largest historical reconstruction in Canadian history.

cod and as a pivotal place of commerce, with a thriving trade in manufactured and other goods imported from France, Quebec, the West Indies, and New England. No sooner had Louisbourg been built than it changed hands when the French could not withstand a siege by British troops in 1745. Although the French regained possession three years later as the result of a treaty, the fort was forcibly turned over a second time to the British

in 1758, when a 150-ship armada carrying 27,000 soldiers and crew demolished the fortress walls. Those walls lay in ruins until they were excavated and reconstructed by Parks Canada beginning in the 1960s. Today, the Louisbourg experience begins with an orientation at a visitor reception centre off-site from the fortress proper. But it is at the fortress gate that the transition begins. Be prepared for an inquisition by "armed" sentries whose job it is

to playfully intimidate, interrogate, and extend a welcome all at the same time. The sentries are just the first of many professional, costumed animators who help bring the authenticity of Louisbourg to life. A highlight of the visit is the King's Bastion, a structure palatial enough to be considered a fort within a fortress, and which in its day was one of the largest buildings in North America. But buildings are only the backdrop in the process of repatriating

history—Louisbourg is about far more than bricks and mortar. Parks Canada has succeeded in enriching the lives of visitors through a wide range of experiences, such as after-dark murder-mystery walks and candlelit dining in the themed tavern. Arguably no location of historical significance in Atlantic Canada has the same dramatic stature as the Fortress of Louisbourg.

Antigonish Highland Games

Where do the visiting heavy event athletes of the Antigonish Highland Games get to sit when they patronize the local town pubs each July? At heights well over 6 feet and averaging 285 pounds (a 2009 Belgian competitor measured in at 6'10" and 340 pounds), the answer is any place they like. "Heavy events" are exactly what their name implies: athletic contests involving the moving or throwing of heavy objects, including stones, hammers, and cabers. (The caber toss is likely the competition most commonly associated with the Scottish.) The "big stick," as the caber is called, is a Nova Scotia red spruce that must be tossed accurately and at the right angle in order to score the most points. Most heavy athletic events come from real Scottish farming tradition. The Challenge Sheaf, for example, is derived from the traditional competition of seeing who could toss a sheaf of wheat the highest. The Highland Games heavy event contests are real crowd-pleasers, but the games are an eclectic mix of many things associated with Scottish heritage, tradition, and culture, including highland dance competitions, piping and drumming, storytelling, a Concert Under the Stars, and tug-of-war contests with teams from across North America. The Antigonish Highland Games is a true institution that reflects the Scottish culture that, from the provincial tartan emblem to the famous Cape Breton Highlands, is so much a part of the fabric of Nova Scotia.

For sheer cultural regalia and bravado, the Antigonish Highland Games is a standout attraction with a long tradition in Atlantic Canada.

Glace Bay Miners' Museum

Some people shudder at the thought of descending into the pit of an Ocean Deeps Colliery. (The collieries are dark landmarks of Cape Breton's coal mining industry, which began in the 1700s to meet the coal-burning needs of the nearby French fortification of Louisbourg.) Coal mining, after all, has always been one of the most dangerous of occupations, with black-faced men working perilously in tunnels reaching far under the ocean floor. But the Glace Bay Miners' Museum experience in northern Cape Breton is devoid of toil and danger. Rather, it is safe, enlightening, and entertaining, and uses artifacts and photographic exhibits to illustrate the development of Cape Breton's once-vast coal fields and the various mining techniques common to the area. It is also one attraction where the guides are living, breathing examples of the stories being showcased. Guides with names like Abbie, Donnie, Wishie, and Sheldon—stalwart men who once worked below—take visitors underground to learn about a job that in 1873 paid from 80 cents to $1.50 per day for miners and 65 cents for trapper boys as young as eight years of age. (Trapper boys opened and closed air control doors when boxes of coal passed.) The guides talk about the companies they worked for, the unions they were loyal to, the equipment they used, and how they risked their lives every time they went underground. The fifteen-acre site includes a replica miner's home, a company store (to which the miners and their families were often beholden), a restaurant, and a gift shop. An absolute highlight is a performance by The Men of the Deeps, a choir of miners whose music will touch your heart and tingle your spine.

Transitioned from one of the most dangerous occupations in the world to friendly tour interpreters, the guides at Cape Breton Island's Glace Bay Miners' Museum are the real deal when it comes to authentic storytelling.

Restaurant Chez Christophe

Creative comfort food and traditional surroundings are the order of the day at Restaurant Chez Christophe on Nova Scotia's Acadian shore.

Acadian roots typically run deep and proud all along Nova Scotia's Evangeline Trail, but nowhere more so than at Restaurant Chez Christophe, where chef Paul Comeau has created a simple yet special culinary world in the home of his great-great-grandfather Christophe Duguas. In fact, the house was referred to locally as Chez Christophe, in deference to the owner, long before Comeau opened the place to the public in 1996. Located along Nova Scotia's French Shore in tiny Gross Coques (which translates as "large clams"), the restaurant is a simple old-fashioned farmhouse, built in 1837, that has undergone a series of modest expansions since its conversion into a commercial establishment. The clams that are the surrounding community's namesake are found on nearby shores where Acadians have harvested them for as long

as anyone can remember. It is this proximity to the ocean and its harvest of fresh seafood that form the lifeblood of Atlantic Canadian communities such as Gross Coques and which set places like Chez Christophe apart from the typical dining experience. Gregarious, mustachioed Comeau prepares and serves only comfort foods, among them authentic Acadian recipes like fricot and rappie pie. He has retained the charm of his family's heritage home with a flavour of early rural Acadian décor, exemplified by mismatched wooden tables and chairs that were typically found in people's homes. Working away in his small kitchen, Comeau has created a genuine sense of down-home, Maritime-Acadian warmth for his customers.

Annapolis Valley Wine Tour

The Annapolis Valley is not Napa Valley, or even the Niagara Region, with countless wineries that blanket the landscape. But, when you combine the emergence of vineyards and wineries with the Annapolis Valley's endless, famed fields of apple orchards, you have a growing travel destination driven by agriculture and entrepreneurial imagination. Domaine de Grand Pré Winery, Gaspereau Vineyards, Blomidon Estate Winery, Sainte-Famille Wines, L'Acadie Vineyards, Benjamin Bridge Vineyards, and Muir Murray Estate Winery—seven of the eleven members of the Nova

Culinary tourism is at its best where wineries tend to cluster, hence the popularity of California's Sonoma Valley and Ontario's Niagara region. Nova Scotia's Annapolis Valley is poised as the new kid on the block as wineries spring up in an agricultural zone where apples once grabbed all the glory.

Scotia wineries association—are all situated in the Annapolis Valley, clearly proclaiming that this is an emerging wine region of note. Each winery is doing its part by growing special varieties of grapes suited to the Atlantic Canadian climate that are sure to please the palates of wine lovers. Varieties include L'Acadie Blanc, Seyval Blanc, Baco Noir, and Leon Millot, all of which have won awards at the annual All Canadian Wine Championships. It's wonderful to visit the boutiques and showrooms of these emerging wineries and to taste their blends

and tour their grounds and facilities, but it is just as wonderful to tour the vineyards, which sit amid the lush, green contours of the Annapolis Valley. The valley wineries have also smartly played an important and active role in the development of two growing events that are attracting new types of customers to the province: the Nova Scotia Fall Wine Festival and the Nova Scotia Winter Icewine Festival (held during February), both of which combine the excellence of local vintners with the fabulous flavours of local chefs.

Bras d'Or Lakes

"Canada's Inland Sea," as the Bras d'Or Lakes have been coined, provides safe passage for sailors and scenic splendour for touring vacationers visiting Nova Scotia's masterpiece, Cape Breton Island.

Writer Silver Donald Cameron described the Bras d'Or Lakes as "a basin ringed by indigo hills laced with marble"; the area, he said, contained "islands within a sea inside an island." The Bras d'Or Lakes is really a singular lake occupying a large mass of territory (one hundred kilometres long by fifty kilometres at its widest point) near the centre of Cape Breton Island. Given its size, the Bras d'Or has quite appropriately been called "Canada's inland sea," and to sailors, in particular, the phrase couldn't be more apt. The lake is large enough to raise a spinnaker, but is generally fog-free and protected enough to make sailing safe, carefree and, because of the countless coves and islands, a very interesting and entertaining place in which to navigate. The Bras d'Or is so popular that it's considered a preferred destination for sailors from around the Maritimes. Travelling the lakes also exposes sailors to nature; situated at the meeting point of the Cape Breton Highlands and lowlands, there are many species of wildlife and birds, including hundreds of pairs of bald eagles that nest in trees along the shoreline. For landlubbers, the Bras d'Or Lakes Scenic Drive, part of the Nova Scotia Scenic Travelways network, loops around the waterway, routing through numerous communities and attractions, including the St. Peters Canal, recording artist Rita MacNeil's Tea Room, and beautiful Baddeck, informally considered the capital of the Bras d'Or region.

Glenora Distillery

No matter where they live or travel, whisky lovers can concoct any number of excuses to stop for a smooth, warm, and woody single malt. Today, Cape Breton Island's Glenora Distillery is on their list. The distillery's suitably branded Glen Breton blend is reputedly North America's only single malt whisky, produced just minutes from the ocean and beaches of western Cape Breton Island. The distillery's proprietors are honest enough to admit that although what they produce is surely Scotch in spirit—Glen Breton is produced in traditional copper pot stills using just barley, yeast, and water—the end product cannot be officially called Scotch if it's not actually produced

in Scotland. Hence Glen Breton's description as a "Rare Canadian Single Malt Whisky." Tours, tastings, souvenirs, and musical ceilidhs (the adjacent Glenora Inn and the distillery are situated, after all, right on the Ceilidh Trail scenic route) all form part of a visit to Glenora, immersing visitors in a true Cape Breton Gaelic cultural experience. And there is one added element that this particular distillery could not dare overlook: As a true Cape Breton distillery, Glen Breton produces private label concoctions of white, amber, and dark rums, the island's most preferred spirits long since the days of rum-runners.

Glenora Distillery's Glen Breton whisky cannot be called Scotch, because technically it is not produced in the Mother Country, but your taste buds will tell you that this single malt blend is every bit as highland as any from Scotland.

Sugar Moon Maple Farm

The proprietors of Sugar Moon Farm are more than maple sugar farmers. They pride themselves just as much on their role as custodians of their local community of Earltown, of their land, and of the local water resource. They buy local with an emphasis on organic products, they employ working draft horses, they're avid composters, and they are continuously managing their woodlots. Located just north of Truro, Sugar Moon Farm is a member of the Atlantic Economuseum network, an umbrella organization recognized for its holistic perspective on retail enterprise and traditional artisans at work. At the heart of the Economuseum philosophy is a high standard of quality throughout the operation. Visitors to Sugar Moon Farm can learn about the history and craft of maple sugaring in a traditional sugar camp setting. But keeping all of their natural surroundings in mind, Sugar Moon proudly takes advantage of nature's year-round offerings, including their Rogart Mountain Trail, a 6.2-kilometre hike that begins and ends in the parking lot, as well as wintertime sleigh rides. In addition to taking Sugar Moon's products home, what visitors really enjoy is the prepared food, with a menu that includes all-you-can-eat organic Red Fife buttermilk pancakes and what they call their Tatamagouche Omelette, named for the nearby Northumberland Strait community.

Economuseums form a network demonstrating traditional craftspeople plying their trade and educating consumers at the same time. Sugar Moon Maple Farm is the only Economuseum in Atlantic Canada whose product focuses on the tradition of Canadian maple syrup harvesting, processing, and tasting.

Cycling the Cabot Trail

With the slow travel movement—especially closer engagement to area communities—so much in vogue these days, the idea of cycling at, or to, one's destination is a popular activity. Cape Breton Island's world famous Cabot Trail is a classic case in point. Sure, there is pain to be endured, but the finer visual details and downhill rewards are to be cherished. It's not necessarily the three hundred kilometres that will challenge you if you dare to attempt the trip. It's the formidable succession of Cape Smokey, North Mountain, French Mountain, and the one locals have nicknamed "the snake"—

MacKenzie Mountain—that together constitute what is arguably the most daunting cycling tour in Atlantic Canada. While most visitors tour the Cabot Trail by vehicle in a counter-clockwise direction in order to drive closer to the most dramatic viewscapes on the trail's west segments, experienced cycling guides recommend doing the loop clockwise in order to take advantage of the often brisk tailwinds. The same guides also recommend making the trip in September when there is less traffic to contend with and the blackflies and mosquitoes are usually gone. But no matter the mode of transport, the Cabot

Not for the faint of heart, cycling Cape Breton's Cabot Trail includes encounters with heavy-duty hills and the winds off the Gulf of St. Lawrence. But as with most challenges in sport and in life, the rewards (in this case the scenery) are more than worth the effort.

Trail is unquestionably one of the most astonishing and best-known road trips in the world, comparable with those in Europe and with California's Big Sur. And the Cabot Trail has one advantage over its rivals: the spectacular kaleidoscope of fall foliage that occurs from late September to the middle or end of October. This explosive transition of nature laid seed to Cape Breton's annual Celtic Colours cultural celebrations, another reason to cycle the trail in the fall—especially since visitors can literally bike from concert to concert.

St. Ann's Gaelic College

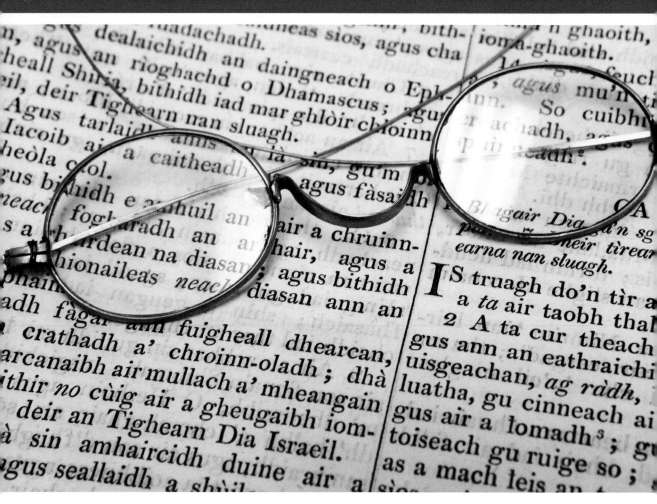

Fàilte dhan a' Cholaisde Ghàidhlig. Thigibh a-staigh! (Welcome to the Gaelic College. Come on in!). The one place outside the United Kingdom where you are most likely to hear the Gaelic language is on Nova Scotia's Cape Breton Island. This is no accident. The Gaelic College of Arts and Crafts in St. Ann's offers formal curricula in accordance with its original 1930s mission statement: "to promote, preserve and perpetuate through studies in all related areas—the culture, music, language, arts, crafts, customs and traditions of immigrants from the Highlands of Scotland." From complete Gaelic immersion to summer courses, March break weekends, and online courses, St. Ann's has come to symbolize for the Celtic heritage interests of Nova

Scotia what the Université Sainte-Anne-Collège de l'Acadie at the opposite end of the province has come to symbolize for the province's French Acadians: the preservation of a minority culture. Studying Celtic culture can be serious business demanding a substantial commitment. At St. Ann's, it can take as long to become a journeyman in the art of kilt-making as it takes to become a doctor. For visitors, there is much more to St. Ann's than the knowledge that there are authentic academic activities taking place in the college's classrooms. The college's museum—the Great Hall of the Clans—tells the stories of the social and military history of Scotland, while the Gaelic College Craft Shop puts a treasure trove of souvenirs and keepsakes on the shelf for those feeling even the

The retention of Gaelic language and related cultural influences—music, dance, and crafts—have an ardent ally in St. Ann's Gaelic College on Cape Breton Island.

Bird Islands, Englishtown

Showcasing bald eagles snatching fish from the ocean, grey seals basking on rocks, and toucan-like "penguins" known as Atlantic puffins—the Bird Islands of Hertford and Ciboux on Cape Breton Island are just a forty-five-minute boat ride from the government wharf at Englishtown. Ironically, "English" town was one of the first places established by the French as a fishing community in 1597, and thirty years later it became Fort Sainte-Anne. The Bird Islands are also the site of the legend of the Glooscap cave, where the Mi'kmaq people believe their spirit Glooscap resides.

Not only is Englishtown still a small active fishing port, but it is also the home of the Englishtown cable ferry, which saves driving time by crossing part of St. Ann's Bay, a worthwhile experience in and of itself. There are a wide variety of seabird species on the two islands, including the great cormorant, whose colony here is said to be more prolific than at any other place in North America. One of the Bird Islands tour services operating from Englishtown is run by the self-proclaimed "puffin lady," Donelda MacAskill, and her husband, a grand-nephew of Cape Breton's world famous giant Angus MacAskill.

Marine excursions leaving from Englishtown, Cape Breton Island, provide up-close encounters with species of marine birds—like the colourful Atlantic puffin—that you just can't get from the land.

(The 7'9", 425-pound MacAskill toured with the Barnum and Bailey Circus and was born, buried, and commemorated in Englishtown.) As part of the puffin lady's on-board interpretation, she loves to tell the story of the Bird Island lighthouse-keeper's wife who used to anchor and tie ropes around her children whenever they played outdoors to ensure they could not fall over the nearby cliff. Danger and living precariously formed part of the natural existence of the resident light-keepers and their families and the mariners who skirted the islands. Today's modern excursions are professionally risk-managed and therefore less precarious, but they are nevertheless full-fledged adventures that only a select few visitors to Atlantic Canada ever take the time and the trouble to experience.

Skyline Trail

The Cabot Trail through Cape Breton Highlands National Park is nothing short of a scenic spectacle, but it can be a fleeting experience when you're within the constant motion of a car or RV. Leaving your vehicle to experience the Skyline Trail will completely alter your perspective on what the Cabot Trail has to offer. Stopping to absorb the winding ribbon of highway made so famous through tourism advertising is really a necessary part of this world-class touring experience. The Skyline Trail is aptly named: it provides stunning vistas of the mountain forests and the Gulf of St. Lawrence

There are city skylines and then there is the view from the Skyline Trail, an iconic stop at Cape Breton Highlands National Park. With seven kilometres of relatively easy hiking, the Skyline provides one of the most accessible nature experiences in Nova Scotia within view of one of the world's most treasured ribbons of scenic highway—the Cabot Trail.

shoreline. Visitors can become so preoccupied with the magic of the Highlands' horizons and viewscapes that the Skyline's seven kilometres of hiking simply melt into a nominal challenge. And there are miracles all around: in spite of salt-laden air and forceful Les Suetes winds whipping down from the Highlands, stunted and twisted trees still manage to grow; whales migrating through the Gulf spray intermittent misty breaths of ocean water; and moose appear out of nowhere, browsing on the new growth of low-lying greenery. The Skyline Trail feels like walking to the edge of the world.

Cape Forchu Light Station

The first light for mariners arriving in Nova Scotia from the United States, Cape Forchu Light Station in southern Nova Scotia is a destination in itself, with a tea room, gift shop, museum, and rocky view-scapes that are every bit as intriguing and picturesque as the significantly more famous Peggy's Cove.

Popular Peggy's Cove gets the lion's share of admiration and attention when it comes to Atlantic Canadian lighthouses, but there are several hundred of the seaside icons spread across the region that, as lighthouses go, are just as worthy. One of the least known but most historically important is the Cape Forchu Light Station near Yarmouth, Nova Scotia. Because it is more remote than its famous Nova Scotia cousin, Cape Forchu (which translates from French as "forked cape") draws a mere fraction of Peggy's Cove's visitors. But visiting Forchu can be a much more personal experience, away from the throngs of people one often finds at Peggy's Cove. Situated near the junction of two of Nova Scotia's most popular scenic travel-ways—the Lighthouse Route and the Evangeline Trail—the cape's solitude is one of its best selling points. Add

in the rocks, the varied elevations, and the ocean, and you have a fantastic place to explore. As the first beacon of light for vessels approaching Canada from the United States, Forchu has had a special role in guiding mariners since 1840. A museum inside the lighthouse tells of lives lost and saved at sea, of the keepers who kept the beacon alight, and of the vital fishing industry in southwest Nova Scotia. Explorer Samuel de Champlain would have appreciated the reassurance of such a light when he encountered and named Cape Forchu in 1604. More than four centuries later, visitors to Forchu can relax in the light-station's tea room while they absorb the heritage offerings of a place that has been protected and preserved by the Friends of the Light, a volunteer group formed in the 1990s to save the property from demolition. Local volunteer

Gary Kent strikes a powerful emotional chord when he describes why he loves Cape Forchu: "To me the Cape Forchu light station holds the power of an exquisitely cut solitaire diamond. You don't need a cluster—one majestic cut holds the power and captures the essence of Mother Nature's beauty and elegance. It's a rare and wondrous moment to be there and experience it." Geography and remoteness, it seems, can be blessings in disguise.

The Kenomee Canyon Trail System offers the most diversified network of hiking—from novice to the most highly skilled—in Nova Scotia.

In response to the 1992 Rio de Janeiro international Convention on Biological Diversity, the province of Nova Scotia designated twenty-eight protected wilderness areas, encompassing more than a quarter of the province's Crown land. One of these, the Economy River Wilderness Area, was chosen because it handsomely represents the diversity of landscapes that transition from the Bay of Fundy into

the Cobequid Uplands. For serious hikers, nothing in Nova Scotia surpasses the diversity and challenge of the eighteen-kilometre Kenomee Canyon Trail, a segment of the greater Kenomee system of four trails that loop through the designated wilderness area. The first trail created within the protected areas network, and according to trail designers still one of the best, the Kenomee Canyon Trail is not for

the faint of heart: it passes near the Economy River gorge and encounters two lakes, four waterfalls, three fjord-type river crossings, as well as a steel span bridge and stone steps above Economy Falls. For overnighters, there are wilderness camping areas in the upper parts of the watershed. However, the overseeing trail society has thought of novice hikers too. The Economy Falls Trail is only 1.0 kilometre long and is classified as easy, while the two other trails, the 6.6-kilometre Devil's Bend Trail

and the 2.5-kilometre Cobequid Escarpment Trail, are listed as moderate challenges. This exceptional diversity of experiences is important because adventurers come in all shapes, sizes, ages, and desires; the challenge, in other words, is in the eye of the beholder. The Kenomee system is one of those special places where trail planners have kept in mind that the market for outdoor destinations can range from people seeking a true wilderness experience, to those who prefer a taste of adventure without inconvenience or risk.

Apple Blossom Festival

The very name conjures up a sense of "Canadiana" as familiar to many as the Quebec Winter Carnival or the Calgary Stampede. And one of the beauties of the Annapolis Valley's premier happening is that it has retained a powerful sense of community and grassroots involvement that makes people return year after year.

The first official Annapolis Valley Apple Blossom Festival was held in 1933 and commemorated more than three centuries of apple farming. The original objectives of staging the Apple Blossom Festival were three-fold: to promote the area's apple-producing industry, to provide an outlet for fostering and developing local talent, and to capitalize on some of Nova Scotia's early tourism initiatives.

Given that the festival takes place over five days beginning on the last Wednesday in May, it is considered by many to represent the start of Nova Scotia's summer. The festival is high on tradition, retaining a popular formula that over the decades has included the hallmarks of many community events in Atlantic Canada, including a grand street parade, fireworks, pancake breakfasts, concerts, and children's events. The community still crowns its Queen Annapolisa, together with her first and second ladies-in-waiting, and a Miss Congeniality, although this is less a beauty pageant than it is a leadership competition among the community's young women. Linked to this competition are a series

of Princess Teas that precede the main festival dates by a week, providing local engagement for the main communities that dot the valley. Most importantly, the festival has never lost the focus of its roots: celebrating local agriculture. Recently, the event has embraced the emergence of local wineries by staging a "Blossoms by the Glass" winery tour and a Food and Wine Expo.

To underscore the festival's national significance and its longevity as it moved into the new millennium, the festival was officially recognized by two national Canadian institutions. In 2001, Canada Post recognized the Apple Blossom Festival as one of the top ten Canadian tourist attractions and created a commemorative stamp marking the festival's sixty-ninth consecutive year of operation. The following year, the Royal Canadian Mint presented the organization with a fifty-cent sterling silver coin struck in its honour. Today the festival remains one of the province's most popular and largest celebrations, with the annual Saturday parade alone drawing tens of thousands of spectators.

Surfing at Lawrencetown

"Chill out" at Lawrencetown Beach is not surfing terminology; it's more like a hypothermia warning. Surfers at this Atlantic surfing mecca have to gear up for the rigours of the frigid North Atlantic Ocean.

It may not be as exotic as Hawaii's famous Ehukai Beach, but Nova Scotia's Lawrencetown Beach has earned rightful recognition around the world as a great surfing destination in Atlantic Canada. A south-facing strand of sand that extends for one and a half kilometres along Nova Scotia's eastern shore, Lawrencetown Provincial Park is just half an hour from the capital city of Halifax. Although surfers can be regularly found at Lawrencetown, the apex of the beach's surf season is the September Storm Classic, a combined amateur and pro event that at times has featured serious purses of up to ten thousand dollars and has attracted competitors from around the world. In surfing vernacular Lawrencetown can attract what are known as "tow-in surfers" who are looking for hurricane-aftermath, twelve-foot Tahitian-style "barrels" as well as beginner-to-average surf hounds in search of more modest waves. For those who do dare to brave the waves in this part of North America, there is one challenge that outstrips that found in the world's greatest surfing destinations: water temperature. While spectators can watch in relative warmth from the beach, the Atlantic Ocean in these parts is generally quite cold, even during a typical Nova Scotia summer. Imagine then that some enthusiasts surf Lawrencetown, as well as nearby Cow Bay and Martinique beaches, in the bone-chilling dead of winter.

Magdalen Islands

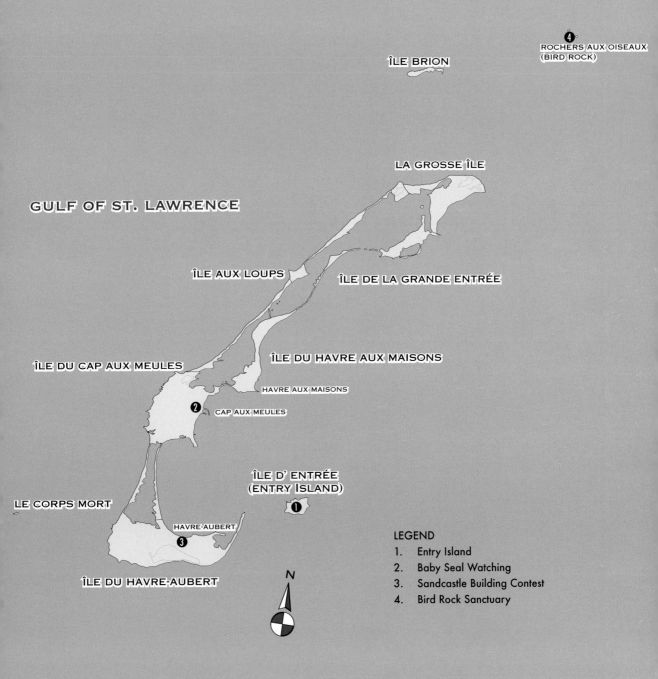

ROCHERS AUX OISEAUX
(BIRD ROCK)

ÎLE BRION

LA GROSSE ÎLE

GULF OF ST. LAWRENCE

ÎLE AUX LOUPS

ÎLE DE LA GRANDE ENTRÉE

ÎLE DU CAP AUX MEULES

ÎLE DU HAVRE AUX MAISONS

HAVRE AUX MAISONS

CAP AUX MEULES

LE CORPS MORT

ÎLE D' ENTRÉE
(ENTRY ISLAND)

HAVRE-AUBERT

ÎLE DU HAVRE-AUBERT

N

LEGEND
1. Entry Island
2. Baby Seal Watching
3. Sandcastle Building Contest
4. Bird Rock Sanctuary

Within the archipelago known as the Magdalen Islands (or in French, Îles de la Madeleine), there are nine major islands, most of which are connected by lengthy sand dune formations created by the winds and the tides of the Gulf of St. Lawrence. Entry Island—with its sheer cliffs in some sections as tall as 170 metres—is the most remote of these, sitting nearly twelve kilometres from the capital of Cap-aux-Meules, and one of three places in the Magdalens that have English-speaking communities. Entry Island's population of between 100 and 150 inhabitants is declining.

Beautiful for its sparseness as much as for its ocean-side setting, Quebec's Entry Island is no doubt one of the least visited islands in the Atlantic region.

Most are descendants of the Dickson and Mclean families from Liverpool, Nova Scotia, who arrived there in 1822. Still connected to their British roots, Entry Islanders have as many friends and relatives in Anglo-Atlantic Canada as in the Magdalens themselves. (And even though there is no geographic or true cultural connection between the two islands, Entry Islanders are noted for strong accents that resemble those in parts of Newfoundland.) It is nothing short of astonishing to sail past Entry Island on board the car ferry from Souris, P.E.I.,

and imagine how determined, resourceful, and resilient those early settlers must have been, not to mention the sparse few who remain today. As in so many other cases of settlement within the Atlantic region, it was the prospects for fishing, primarily lobster, that first attracted settlers there and has permitted those clinging to the community to remain. Today, the ocean harvest is focussed upon Gulf of St. Lawrence crab, scallops, mackerel, herring, and bluefin tuna.

Baby Seal Watching

It has long been fashionable for movie stars and environmental activists to visit the Magdalen Islands to have their photograph taken with the white baby harp seals of the Gulf of St. Lawrence. Anyone else with enough pocket change can do so too, flying from Quebec City to the capital, Cap-aux-Meules, where each March more than a quarter million harp seals complete their migration from Greenland to the gulf to bear their newborns on the massive ice floes found between Prince Edward Island and the Magdalens. In contrast to the global controversy over the harvesting of seal pup fur, the excursions to see the species in their natural habitat are perceived to be a good news story. Small groups of tourists, pampered by warm boots and expedition suits, fine accommodations, meals, and free time for local craft shopping, are shown audiovisual presentations on the subject and flown by helicopter to the floes. The excursions can also include peripheral winter activities such as snowshoeing and dogsledding, but at a promised 96 percent success rate of seeing the pups up close (only bad weather conditions can disrupt the prospects for success), the other activities are merely diversions or value-added experiences for the main event: being able to touch the pups, take photos, and return home with the bragging rights of witnessing, first-hand, one of nature's great spectacles.

Embraced and promoted by celebrities the world over as the elite alternative to the annual Atlantic seal harvest, excursions to the Gulf of St. Lawrence ice floes to view white baby seal pups are among the most expensive and exclusive wildlife adventures in Eastern Canada.

Sandcastle-Building Contest

The Magdalen Islands, five hours by ferry from Souris, P.E.I., but part of the province of Quebec, are a combination of green hills, red sandstone capes, and seemingly endless beaches. It's no accident, then, that the Havre-Aubert Beach, also known as the Sandy Hook, is home to one of the world's best-known sandcastle-building contests (upscale *Coastal Living* magazine places the contest number seven in the world's top ten sandcastle contests). The Magdalen Islands contest is different from similar ones held around the world in that, except for a "Freestyle Division," the sculptures must be of castles and not of humans, beasts, or other figures. Because it is such an internationally regarded competition, some contestants have come

to be quasi-professional sculptors. For novices, however, there are sandcastle technique workshops in the competition lead-up, which takes place on day one of the three-day celebration (although, be warned, the journeymen are an extremely talented lot).

In truth, competitive sandcastle-building is just another excuse to visit what is clearly one of the most exotic places in Atlantic Canada (even if the Magdalens are officially part of Quebec, their geography suggests otherwise). It's thanks to the shifting of the planets that the Magdalens are so frequently associated with great beaches; they were originally situated near what today is the Equator. Millions of years later, the archipelago forms nine

The craftspeople behind these sculptures use more than a pail and a shovel; they employ finesse, ingenuity, and just the right ratio of sand to water.

islands, six of which are connected by expansive sand spits. The surfaces of these long strands of beach are dramatically shaped and altered by Gulf of St. Lawrence winds, which have created the dunes —called "buttereaux" by the French—that can reach up to fifteen metres in height. So while humans have been busy building sandcastles only lately, Mother Nature has been shaping the beaches of the Magdalens since long before recorded time.

Bird Rock Sanctuary

Bird Rock Sanctuary is far from convenient. Even in a high-speed Zodiac, the trip to visit this speck of an island in the middle of the Gulf of St. Lawrence can take more than an hour. Usually conducted in the capable hands of excursion company owner Nadine, the trip takes you from the dock in the Magdalen Islands' Havre-aux-Maisons, to Ile Brion, and then on to Bird Rock, a refuge for large colonies of various avian species, including petrels, northern gannets, razorbills, murres, and the ever-present gulls. The island was inhabited by lighthouse keepers as early as 1870, when it became the first light in the Magdalen Islands archipelago, but today it is abandoned, with signals in this important shipping lane now provided by an automated light. Sheer cliffs reaching more than five hundred feet above sea level make Bird Rock generally inaccessible except by helicopter. There are, however, the remnants of a rusted old steel track running from the cliff's edge to the surface of the water, presumably installed to lift the light keeper and his provisions to the top. In such a

It's a lengthy boat ride to a place where you can't even land, and that's part of Bird Rock Sanctuary's cachet. The cliffs are so vertical and daunting that this marine excursion encircles the island rather than challenge it.

harsh and dangerous environment, it's hard to imagine how it was constructed and installed, let alone dwelled upon. Today, Bird Rock Sanctuary is administered by the Canadian Wildlife Service under the Migratory Birds Convention Act and the Canadian Wildlife Act, making it official: the site is an important natural asset to Canada's migratory bird population and important, therefore, to Canadians. The designation also sends a signal to nature lovers and adventurers that the sanctuary is a true standout among Atlantic Canada's nature-based experiences.

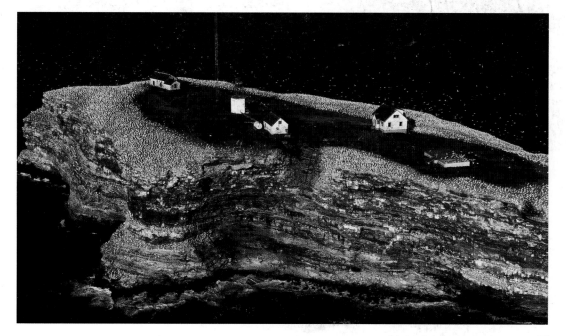

Photo Credits

All photos are copyright George Fischer except the following:

Pascal Arseneau, page 80
Claude Bouchard, page 47
Dolores Breau, page 34, 81, 89 (top), 96, 97, 98, 102, 104, 105, 160, 161, 162, 172, 173, 196, 197, 199
Brian Bursey, page 110, 111, 136, 137, 138, 139, 140, 141, 142, 143, 144, 145
Crown Jewel Resort, page 150, 151 (top), 189

Ryan Fischer, page 37, 159 (bottom), 169, 181
Sean Fischer, page 68, 70, 71, 74, 75, 76, 77, 78, 79, 82, 83, 88, 89 (bottom), 92, 93, 99, 100, 101, 106, 107, back cover
Donald R. LeBlanc, page 163
Tourism New Brunswick, page 22, 23, 58, 59, 60, 61
Tourism Nova Scotia, page 156, 157, 176, 177, 178, 179, 192, 193, 204, 205, 221
Len Wagg, page 222, 223

Acknowledgements

This book would not have been possible without the generous support of our Canadian partners and sponsors. In particular, I would like to express my gratitude to Randy Brooks and Pamela Wamback at the Nova Scotia Department of Tourism, Culture, and Heritage; Mike Taylor and Garrett Turta at the Fairmont Algonquin Hotel; Diane Rioux at Tourism New Brunswick; Marc Deschenes at ViaRail Canada; and Robert Ferguson and Carol Horne at Tourism Prince Edward Island.

For safely flying me to and fro, thanks to Robert Bourque of the Debert Flight Centre, Nick Harding of Eastern Air Services, and Gregor Allison of Crown Jewel Aviation.

I would also like to thank the following individuals for modelling for me: James Miller and Sierra Stoddard at the Old Triangle in Halifax; John Riddell at the Cape Forchu lighthouse; Brook, Meredith, and Seth Marks; Elizabeth Yorke, Justin Yorke, Robbie Smith, and Roger, Susan, and Dakota McAloney; Daniel, Christine, Halaina, Connor, and Ava Basham; and Sheldon McNeil at the Glace Bay Miners' Museum.

For providing me with logistic and tour support I would like to thank Diane Lombard at the Ganong Chocolate Museum; Joanne and Rob Carney of Tall Ship Whale Adventures; Darcy Snell of The Lighthouse on Cape d'Or; Captain John Bryson of Amoeba Sailing Tours; Donelda MacAskill of Donelda's Puffin Boat Tours; Nahman Korem and Iris Kedmi at Crown Jewel Resort; and Daniel MacLean at the Glenora Distillery.

For accommodations and transportation, thanks to Thrifty car rental, Hertz car rental, Delta Halifax, White Point Beach Resort, Brier Island Lodge, Hillsdale House, Tidal Bore Rafting Park and Cottages, Gillespie House Inn, Joggins Fossil Centre, Haus Treuburg Country Inn, Dundee Resort, and the Fairmont Algonquin Hotel.

To fill in gaps for areas that I did not have time to photograph I would like to thank my sons, Sean and Ryan Fischer, and my good friends Dolores Breau, Donald Leblanc, Pascal Arseneau, and Claude Bouchard.

As always thanks to my great assistants: Jean Lepage, Sean and Ryan Fischer, and Harvey Sawler for writing the great text.

—GF

The hundreds of people within the Atlantic Canada tourism industry whom I have dealt with over the past three decades are exceptional people who are in love with where they live and work, as am I. Tourism has been good to me. I would particularly like to thank some of my greatest industry friends and advocates over the years, including Francis McGuire, Dave Lough, Don Groom, Lawrence MacPherson, Rory Beck, Chip Bird, Real Robichaud, the late William J. Hancox, and the late David Rodd. Most of all I would like to thank my partner, Charlotte Stewart, who is the ultimate travelling planner and companion.

—HS